*This book has been independently
published on amazon.com platform by
Aysel Mammadova
ayselmammadova@protonmail.com*

ISBN: 9798326289759

Copyright © Aysel Mammadova 2024

*All rights reserved. This publication may not be reproduced, stored
in a retrieval system or transmitted, in any form or by any means,
electronic, mechanical, photocopying, recording or otherwise,
without prior permission of the publisher.*

About the author:

In this book, looking through the prism of his own experience, the author discusses the reliability of the Council of Europe's protections against politically motivated arrest and sentencing in a member state. Ilgar Mammadov is the leader of the Republican Alternative (REAL) Party, which opposes what it calls "the ongoing erosion of the republican foundations of the Azerbaijani state". Between 2012 and 2019 he spent five and a half years in prison, but in 2020 the country's Supreme Court acquitted Mammadov of all charges in a long delayed decision in accordance with his unprecedented landmark victory at the European Court of Human Rights. In the February 2020 elections, the REAL Party was recognized as winning only one out of a total of 125 parliamentary seats, while international observers criticized the polls for violations, such as the exclusion of Mammadov from all ballots since 2013.

ILGAR MAMMADOV

THE COUNCIL OF EUROPE
When Icarus Followed the Flight Instructions

2024

WHY THE BOOK?

A renowned Russian historian of Turkic civilizations, Lev Gumilev, is believed to have said that the Turks achieved the greatest victories in human history, but they barely cared about hiring a chronicler to record them.

After spending almost six years in prison, I had been handling my unprecedented success at the European Court of Human Rights very much in that modest Turkic manner. This lasted for years – until a light bulb moment at a conference in Vilnius in November 2023. At a late-night session, an Armenian diplomat was given the closing slot to speak about the democratic aspirations of his nation. He did so pretty well, but at the end of his presentation he accused my country of wrongs we had never committed. I was upset by the pressing need to respond at such a late hour to the audacity of his blatant falsehood. At my insistence, the session ended with my commentary – polite, but very uncomfortable for the diplomat.

As participants were leaving the conference room after the event, he approached me and hurled a tirade in my direction, of which the only intelligible part was a claim that in a private conversation with him, a senior Council of Europe official had called me 'the greatest disappointment'. This bilious accusation assumed disproportion between the support the Council had provided to me in detention and my gratitude.

That was the moment I decided to pen this book. Not only because I suspected the diplomat might be relaying accurate information, but also because I felt I must beat that nonchalant ancient Turk residing inside myself.

Comparatively, Turkic stories are overloaded with verbs, and are poor in adjectives because their aesthetics lie in depicting actions more than in enriching the vocabulary of contemplation. Mine will be no exception.

This book is not about the fears and horrors of time in prison. It is not about the remarkable people you can befriend within those walls. It will not dwell on what you feel in the last period of your sentence when you do not know if your term will be extended or not, and if you should anticipate a beating or poisoning at the weekend. That kind of story has been eloquently told in many other books by people with greater literary talents.

This book will help you discover the reliability of the Council of Europe's protections against politically motivated arrest and sentencing in a member state.

WHAT WAS NOT BEHIND IT ALL

A great many people believed for a long time that on 4 February 2013 I was arrested because of a live televised debate in which I dared to accuse President Ilham Aliyev of treading the same path as the Iranian shah overthrown in 1979. Astonishingly, even today, every taxi driver who starts up a political conversation with me staunchly believes that he watched the speech unfold in real time. It is nothing less than the Mandela effect: nearly four years passed between that TV debate, unnoticed by the general public at the time, and my scandalous arrest. Most people watched it only in 2015, when after almost a decade of an oil revenue boom two waves of currency devaluation hit the Azerbaijani economy hard, making everyone poorer, and thus heightening the popular demand for opposition perspectives.

My reference to Mohammed Reza Shah Pahlavi in that debate was both spontaneous and not. Several years prior to that, I had met a former senior *New York Times* correspondent, a rather arrogant, but clever man named Stephen Kinzer. He was writing a book about Iranian pre-revolutionary politics, and came to converse with my party leader. I was deputy chairman of the National Independence Party in 1998-2003. I am afraid to accidentally misrepresent his views here, but one could sense his disdain for the repressive character of the shah's regime. He considered it to be the main cause of the 1979 theocratic revolution. Mr Kinzer was convincing because he assigned more of a meaning to what was happening in that year, unlike the dry Soviet historiography that was too mindful of relations with Iran. His view as a reporter and political scientist made a greater impact on my understanding of the events than the history department of my alma mater – Lomonosov Moscow State University, which at the time had unique strengths in areas less affected by current affairs.

The debate was broadcast live on a private TV channel the day after the 18 March 2009 referendum, which lifted the term limits on the presidency. Procedurally, it was a farce, not a poll. Four months earlier, unaware of the upcoming referendum, we had founded the Republican Alternative Movement. We stood up for republicanism in the face of an encroaching dynastic reign. Moments before we went on air in the TV studio, I decided to illustrate my opposition to the removal of presidential term limits by using the catchy term 'shah' – in order to emphasize our republican ideology. Luckily, the speech did not go viral, and I avoided detention. It was not aired in prime time, and the Internet had not yet taken over the legacy media. Only the political class of Baku talked about it for a while.

Fast forward to 2018. The old opposition attributed my reluctance to reiterate the comparison between Pahlavi and Aliyev after my release to alleged secret collusion with the government or even to cowardice. Both of these interpretations pleased the government very much, as if it had purposely injected them into the discreditation narrative.

As I have explained publicly on several occasions, by dragging our party into such a conversation, the government wanted to poison our political ties with the US in today's completely different geopolitical environment. Indeed, Pahlavi had been known as a dictator most loyal to the United States. We republicans could criticize Aliyev in that context once, two or three times, but turning this stance into our political trademark might raise eyebrows in America as to what our party's intentions and geopolitical preferences might be. Maintaining such a trademark would be particularly improper after the years of campaigning by the American government and activists for the release of our unjustly incarcerated party members.

Many other people believed that my arrest stemmed from the supposed insult I had directed towards parliament members in November 2012, just three months prior to being indicted. In a pamphlet-styled blog post, I had blasted the legislative amendment drastically increasing penalties for unauthorized street rallies. I compared the parliament to a medieval court zoo, in which Asian despots would dispose of dissenters by feeding them to predators.

The amendment further clipping the already limited freedom of assembly was proposed in the context of the Arab spring, but for me it had a personal dimension too: the bill was nominally authored by Rafael Jabrayilov who had defeated me in the 2010 sham parliamentary elections, whitewashed by the Council of Europe observers.

Although he was previously a prosecutor, one could hardly call Jabrayilov a law-abiding citizen. Actually, he died in jail in 2021. According to media reports on his criminal case, he used his member of Parliament ID as a pawn, literally, to borrow money on the informal market for his poorly run business. Due to these reports, and the subsequent criminal investigation, he lost his seat in autumn 2019, got arrested, and then died of a respiratory virus.

In 2012 that fate of his was years away. He and dozens of other MPs threatened me with a defamation lawsuit for the 'zoo' posting. From the legal point of view, that was a non-starter, and soon the matter faded out. Not least thanks to the European Commission Vice-President Neelie Kroes, whom I met in Baku around the same time. Briefed in advance by her staff, she asked me if one of the MPs named Adil Aliyev had really called for my head to be chopped off. I confirmed the incident. Then she met journalists and condemned these public attacks.

Soon afterwards German Ambassador Herbert Quelle invited me for another routine political conversation. While greeting me, he asked if I would permit him to write an open letter to Adil Aliyev. I advised him not to do so because the issue was disappearing from the press, Adil Aliyev was more restrained in his media appearances, and I did not want the issue to re-surface.

Not every European official displayed the same level of responsiveness. As an opposition politician facing government intimidation, I approached Dunja Mijatović, OSCE representative on freedom of the media, to make her acquaintance during a break at a freedom of speech round table in Baku. However, I learned from her angry reply that I should have requested a meeting instead of approaching her on the sidelines of an event. Well, I quietly disappeared so that madame did not lose her emotional balance. That was two months before the arrest.

Later in November in Canada, I saw Ambassador Peter Semneby, who between 2006 and 2011 served as EU special representative for the South Caucasus. I did not mention to Peter the parliamentarians' irate reactions. Instead, he asked me an intriguing follow-up question about an episode that had happened back in 2010. His unexpected inquiry sparked a thought-provoking exchange between us.

We had had many conversations during his time in office. One occurred shortly after the 2010 parliamentary elections. At a very early breakfast he told me that at nine o'clock he was going to see the president. In advance of that meeting he wanted to hear a quality assessment of the past elections. I provided an overview, and illustrated it with facts from several constituencies, including the one where I personally had been a candidate. At the time, my formal complaint was in review. There was a chance that the voting results could be rectified or even annulled. Nevertheless, I did not ask him to lobby for me at the meeting.

In a week or so, I learned that he had taken the initiative to bring up my name there. First, he did so when delegations were present. An hour later, when the meeting continued in a one-to-one format, he repeated the request, only to be met with Aliyev's evident displeasure.

I was unsure about the type of 'displeasure' being referred to. Now, in 2012 in Canada, he started our conversation by asking, 'Ilgar, did you experience any pressure as a result of my conversation with the president about you?' There was none, honestly, and I told him so.

On second thoughts, Semneby's slightly disturbed appearance made me reconsider some of the recent developments, in search of the potentially underlying rancour.

What recent developments?

ALARM BELLS IGNORED

In October 2012, exactly one year before the presidential elections, I was approached by the government through a channel that I will not risk disclosing even now. The warning I received was clearly worded: 'Do not run for president in next year's elections.'

It was a one-way communication. I could not reply. They could only watch my moves. I received two more warnings before the arrest. Let me explain why.

The plan of our Republican Alternative was to nominate me for presidential elections, achieve a high level of popular recognition of our organization, and then try for success in the 2015 parliamentary elections. We had been planning this with little regard to the warning, of which only a limited circle among our leadership was aware. We did not take it very seriously. We understood how politically and even economically costly it would be for the government to lock me up, given the domestic and international profile of REAL as a voice of the most progressive and educated part of our society.

It appears the government was suspicious about our obvious plan, thinking we were part of a more cunning plot of the West.

We warned the traditional opposition parties that if their alliance failed to nominate a candidate by the end of 2012, the Republican Alternative would nominate me automatically, and we would run a separate campaign from them.

The alliance of traditional opposition parties had a bizarre link to a group of Russian oligarchs of Azerbaijani origin. The group was slowly and undecidedly promoting the presidential candidacy of a prominent film director Rustam Ibragimbekov. The traditional opposition parties had largely discredited themselves by decades of mistaken strategies. They continued to be famous for their infighting more than for providing any credible alternative. Still, we at the newly founded Republican Alternative had no choice other than to accept their candidate if there was one, but only by a certain deadline.

Once they missed the deadline, in January 2013, I declared that I would be running for president that year. On 4 February 2013, I was arrested. The fabricated charges linked me to the organisation of mass spontaneous riots in a provincial city on 23 January.

THE EUROPEAN GENERATION

By 2013 I had been a public figure for about 15 years. From day one, Azerbaijan's drift towards and then formalized membership of the Council of Europe had encouraged my commitment to continue as an opposition politician. Without its protections – now better to say 'perceived protections' – it would have been insane to pursue such a career in my country. The full realization of how insane that was came later, after years behind bars.

Initially, my energy was based on a naïve belief. I thought that the enormous volume of talk about human rights and the rule of law we had heard from European institutions could contain only a small dose of sheer incompetence, corruption and hypocrisy. The level of contamination I discovered along the way was a true revelation.

When handcuffed, I had no less energy, but its source was a different flame. I told myself that you must force the European promise to work, even against its own will. I had no other option than to kiss the sleeping beauty and see what might result.

EARLY DAYS OF UNFREEDOM

As soon as four weeks after the arrest, my application to the European Court of Human Rights was in Strasbourg. It was in English because, I presumed, translation from Azerbaijani could lead to loss of precious weeks. Down the years I learned from others' experience how translation added six and more months to the duration of review. Thank God, I was not aware about this dangerously disheartening calculus then.

Speedy judgment was not my only objective. I feared that upon secret orders from the government, 'errors' might be deliberately inserted into the translations. During my political career, I had seen instances of international election observation missions being sabotaged by 'accidental' misinterpretation of just one key word at a crucial public presentation. Hence, I was taking no chances.

I translated and organized all the texts prepared by my key lawyer Fuad Aghayev, and added a number of points and facts that he believed were not necessary. To my joy, the Court did refer to most of those when following its logical path to conclusion. Fuad has exceptional professional qualities and integrity, but I doubt lawyers would often go an extra mile to explore an opportunity. They are too past dependent. Trying, experimenting was my focus and my job throughout the whole process.

Fuad's brilliant insights into the nature of the European Convention educated me quickly, but also heated up our arguments. Nevertheless, we co-authored a very thorough complaint, with its gem being our claim about violation of Article 18 of the European Convention on Human Rights.

Here I need to explain the peculiar properties of that Article. The criminal law of any country prohibits citizens from performing certain actions – under threat of punishment by the government. The European Convention works the other way. It prohibits governments preoccupied with catching and prosecuting an alleged criminal from performing certain actions. Specifically, Article 18 prohibits them from detaining and putting on trial a defendant for any reason different from the one stated in the indictment. The idea is simple: governments should have no hidden motives. It is worse if the motive can be found in party politics. That makes the detainee a political prisoner.

Fuad has full credit for putting the reference to the breach of the Article into the application. He said the chances of consideration of our claim were low, because by then Article 18 had been applied only four times – in the cases of one Russian, one Moldovan and two Ukrainian citizens. All were high profile public figures. He honestly believed that the Court would only bother looking at Article 18 if the judges were in the mood. Perceptions about the Court's subjectivity and even corruption were very strong not only within the government, but even among human rights lawyers in Azerbaijan. The most moderate gossip I had personally heard from a highly knowledgeable person in Strasbourg said that every judge had an unspoken, that is tolerated, inclination to 'hear' the head of their own state, but only once per judicial term. In extremely important cases that could be a game changer.

Yet, I felt neither that cynical, nor that lucky to leave everything to chance. Therefore, I almost forced Fuad to add a facts-based logical narrative in support of our claim about Article 18. In return, I dropped my insistence on Article 10 of the Convention, which was about guarantees to free speech, and we crossed it out of the application.

I pressed Fuad so hard and had been generally cautious about every legal detail for one more reason. In the second half of the 2000s I had met a prominent lawyer, Jeremy McBride, who spoke to our small group of activists about the European Court of Human Rights. The next month I forgot most of what we'd heard from him, but one thing I remembered forever. He underlined a thought totally alien to the 'liberal democratic' civil society crowd living off international anti-authoritarianism grants. As he said it, Jeremy reinforced it with a shrewd glance at the audience: 'The governments are extremely clever in the Court. Never underestimate what they can do to you there.' I felt this was the only lesson he wanted us to draw from his lecture.

Jeremy's advice was planted in very fertile soil in my head. I already knew too well that the Azerbaijani liberal democratic community had been influenced by a fallacy of Russian liberal tradition, which perceived any authoritarian government as a sort of laughable idiot. To illustrate this

Russian cultural inheritance, it is enough to say that up to the mid-2000s the best selling political newspaper in Azerbaijan was produced in Russian, and practically all impactful online discussions were still held in Russian. Unconsciously adhering to that tradition, most of those who stood up against authoritarianism in our country considered themselves, often for no reason, intellectually superior to the regime. Just like in Russia or, for example, in Belarus. Stories belittling Lukashenko that I had heard from Belarusian activists had always been particularly creative and funny, but pointless in the absence of a serious strategic alternative. You cannot beat an authoritarian government by believing that your sarcasm or sense of moral superiority can substitute for your intelligent action.

Opposition circles in Azerbaijan had the same 'attitude'. In my subjective view, an international political round table around the year 2008, attended by young professionals both from the government and 'liberal' civil society, provided a visual example of it. Whereas the government people participated fully in the event, listening to every speaker and taking notes, the liberal group was practically absent because it was absorbed by just another topic in its social media ghetto, where it could practice its moralizing tone without confronting real life.

Ironically, in 2018 Jeremy McBride contacted us offering his services. He had no idea that we had met some ten years earlier. We instantly took him on board, and he helped to write or polish some of my quarterly letters to the Committee of Ministers.

DIPLOMATIC ROUND BEGINS

The inconveniences of daily life in jail aside, the first month I was busy preparing the application, as described above. In the meantime, international organizations, and western governments continued to issue statements of concern over my detention.

I quickly realized that those statements had only one practical value: we could quote them in our papers sent to the European Court of Human Rights when we needed to remind them of my status as a public figure acting in the public interest, and the government's possession of a motive to silence me.

The limited scope of application of those statements made me recall two old jokes.

The first one was an elitist Russian verbal cartoon about the diplomatic corps. It described someone who had graduated from the Moscow State Institute of International Relations, majoring in Grave Concern as a subject at the Department of Concern.

The other joke was a rustic one. I had heard it in 2010, after another blatantly falsified parliamentary election, from a political candidate who had competed in a rural province. As the story goes, once upon a time, there was Tiger. He often raped Wolf, who finally ended up complaining to Lion, the king of the wild life. At the trial, Lion asked how often the violence occurred. Both sides agreed that it was a weekly practice. The king ruled that from now on Tiger could rape Wolf only once a month. The latter felt a little relieved. However, the evil practice continued most weeks. Every time this happened, Tiger told him to record the incident as a use of the next month's quota. A year later the king suddenly saw Wolf looking very grumpy. The king asked about his life after the ruling. Wolf replied: 'Your Majesty, life is no different, only the volume of paperwork has increased.'

FIRST CONVERSATION

Exactly two months after my arrest, Roland Kobia, head of the EU permanent delegation to Baku, visited me in jail. Actually, we sat down in a big meeting room where with a furtive expression he handed me a piece of paper with a short handwritten text on it: 'Do you think they are filming us?' I answered in the affirmative, but as if this paper was about something else.

Before the arrest we had met frequently, and maintained friendly contact. His style, rich in witty humour, was that of a perfect friend. We last met in December, when a crowd of Azerbaijani civil society activists had attacked him online for his praise of President Aliyev, while I defended him, also publicly. I had argued that by noting whatever the president did well now, he had been trying to put the EU in a position to effectively criticize the next year's presidential elections, if they went particularly wrong.

So now, seven months before the vote, things were already going very badly precisely because of my attempt to run as a candidate, and the EU ambassador was sitting in front of me in jail, describing his very recent conversation with President Aliyev. Roland said they had talked about me for 20 minutes, and the president said only positive things. 'Then what are we doing here?' became the obvious question, but I did not ask it, thinking that Roland had probably assumed the role of a harbinger of good news.

The next day I appealed for bail. That appeal was quickly turned down. Moreover, three weeks later I was indicted for even graver crimes, which later resulted in a more severe sentence. Soon after, Roland Kobia received a new appointment, to another gas giant, Myanmar, and left the country. He occasionally sent me letters of support, for which I was very thankful as they cheered me and my family up.

ABORTED FIRST ACTION

I believe it was early in May that my wife came to tell me that Piotr Świtalski, director for policy planning at the

Council of Europe, had rung her personally to tell her of the Council's firm intention to cancel Azerbaijan's half-year chairmanship of the Committee of Ministers which was to commence in a year: 'The decision is final. We are already finalizing the papers! The decision can only be reversed by Ilgar's release,' he declared with an excitement my wife tried her best to convey to me.

I had known Piotr since 2011, when he became supervisor of the Council of Europe Schools of Political Studies. In 2007-2013 I had managed the Baku 'school' part time, which was in fact a networking programme. It brought together dozens of mid-career politicians, journalists, business people and civil society activists at a series of quarterly seminars, culminating in an annual big gathering of all the schools in Strasbourg. He had even visited our three-day event in Baku once.

His confidence in the cancellation of the chairmanship helped me withstand the particularly strong pressure put on my family throughout summer 2013, such as the criminal case against my wife for an alleged attempt to sneak a mobile phone into the remand facility. Against the background of that case the government tried to force me to write a plea for a pardon to the president. I refused, time and again, and eventually they gave up, and dropped the case against her.

As for the chairmanship, Azerbaijan did become the chair of the Committee of Ministers. By then, Świtalski himself had been called back to his native Polish Foreign Ministry. Soon, in 2015 he became the head of the EU permanent delegation to Armenia until 2019.

This is what he wrote on his blog in November 2022 most probably about his attempt at the Council of Europe to get me released:

'When I took up the post of Head of Political Planning Directorate at the Secretariat, I tried to make my colleagues more principled. Unsuccessfully. "We cannot influence the situation in Russia, Azerbaijan or Turkey anyway. No pressure will help." – I heard. But it was not about efficiency, but about the elementary credibility of the organization, its political prestige.'

We did not make any attempt to see each other, or get in touch after my release. I know what he felt after that incident, and I did not want to disturb him with a negative trip down memory lane.

OTHER INTERNATIONAL ACTIVITIES BEFORE THE TRIAL

By mid-summer 2013 the Council of Europe had surrendered to the government's position that I would be tried in the local court, and no release before then was possible. 'Indeed, how can a member government of such a respected institution as ours lie so blatantly? Ilgar has probably done something wrong, which makes the government so confident. Let's continue business as usual, and we will see eventually,' this is how I reconstruct the thinking in Strasbourg just a few months after my arrest.

In early June, the co-rapporteurs for Azerbaijan from the Monitoring Committee of the Parliamentary Assembly of the Council of Europe came to see me in jail. This needs a context for people who are not aware of Council practices. All relatively new member states of the Council undergo long years of monitoring by this organization regarding their compliance with membership obligations. Visits to detention centres are part of the monitoring routine.

In 2013, by the 12th anniversary of accession to the Council, several co-rapporteurs had already become political celebrities. About half of them had been evil characters in the state-controlled TV news and commentary saga. Some were portrayed neutrally. The rest, such as Yevgeniya Zhivkova, had even been celebrated by the government.

In that account, Pedro Agramunt of Spain and Joseph Debono Grech of Malta had been dark horses, even though both had already spent years as co-rapporteurs on Azerbaijan. So, now I had an opportunity to make a first-hand judgment about their performance.

I was seated at a conference room table, opposite the guests, and started the conversation by thanking them for the statement made right after my arrest. Mr Agramunt hastily interrupted me: 'So, now we are here to hear you.' After that invitation, I spoke for 10-15 minutes about the political motive in the case, referencing some of the articles I had already written from jail. When I finished, the blank-faced Agramunt voiced a dry 'Thank you, we will take note of this presentation.' That signalled the end of the meeting.

I stood up and walked towards the exit, obviously disappointed by the attitude. Suddenly, a lady from the Secretariat of the Parliamentary Assembly who was accompanying the co-rapporteurs, rushed to me to ask if I had access to the Internet and an e-mail address. The silliness of the question only added to my frustration. Probably she felt that and added, as if making excuses: 'You spoke about your articles, so I wanted to know if we can communicate via the Internet.'

The transition to the next scene was instant. Debono Grech quickly approached me and embraced me without saying a word, with the body language of a father embracing his son in the Middle East or Caucasus and with the smile of a Christian preacher. That was weird, and after the meeting I tried to work out the meaning of his gesture – without success before our next meeting the following year.

Two other episodes in June were slightly more encouraging. I was contacted by members of the European

Parliament who had drafted a resolution on my case, and were going to adopt it on 13 June – just a coincidence – one day before my birthday. Called 'The case of Ilgar Mammadov', the resolution became a broader document on the human rights situation in Azerbaijan. I edited the draft a little, correcting references to some facts, and added a call for sanctions against Azerbaijani officials. At the outset, the latter had been missing. Only an expression of concern, and calls on 'the Azerbaijani authorities to step up their efforts to reform'.

What 'efforts to reform'? I was a little puzzled, although mostly happy about the document screaming my name. A week later I realized that the resolution was timed to give extra reason for European Commission President José Manuel Barroso to speak with President Aliyev about human rights during the latter's visit to Brussels on 21 June – particularly, if he was too stubborn on energy and geopolitical matters.

Apparently, he was, because the first question he had to answer at the joint press conference with Barroso was this one from the Radio Free Europe/Radio Liberty reporter Rikard Jozwiak: 'How can you be sure that the election due in October of this year will be free, fair and transparent if we consider that one of your political opponents, Mr Mammadov, is under arrest?'

I watched the conference on TV, and could not miss Aliyev and Barroso giggling together when the reporter said the second question on the same topic would go to the president of the European Commission.

Aliyev was firm in his reply:

'First of all, I'd like to say that none of my political opponents are in prison. This is absolutely wrong information. At the same time, I'd like to tell you that there are no political prisoners in Azerbaijan, if you read carefully the comments after the session of the

Parliamentary Assembly of the Council of Europe this January, which rejected the report about political prisoners of Azerbaijan. I think that this chapter is closed.'

Technically, he was right. I was being held on remand rather than in prison. Semantics matter. You do not want to make an argument with the president of a sovereign state who has just answered your question, do you? Secondly, I was charged with crimes in connection to events that had taken place exactly the same day, only a few hours after the Parliamentary Assembly of the Council of Europe had voted down the resolution on political prisoners in Azerbaijan. It was then that the president felt he had got a strong and lasting mandate from the Council of Europe to settle political scores.

Yet, all these recent developments were good for my morale at the time. Świtalski's push about the chairmanship of the Committee of Ministers, the resolution of the European Parliament and the press conference with the first question about me – all these facts combined did not foreshadow at all that I would remain behind bars for the next five years.

Were I aware of other facts, I would have been more sober though. Responding to the above developments, the administration of the pre-trial detention facility moved me from a single to a multi-person cell, where the second operation to coerce me to write a plea for pardon began. In between, I was held for a week in the punishment cell, but the authorities denied this, saying I had merely been quarantined.

Oh, I forgot to tell you about my cellmates since February. The first week it was a young bureaucrat from a rural social protection centre, charged seven months earlier with corruption in a scandalous case known to me from the news. He was a kind person, with a sharp sense of humour, which helped me to overcome the fears of the early days. His ability to remain cheerful after seven months in custody (which seemed crazy to me back then) was very inspiring. Then he disappeared.

The next week or so I spent alone in the cell. Then they brought a middle-aged man, who, as he said, was charged with possession of a small amount of marijuana. After a week of conversations, I came to the logical conclusion that he was a snitch. Therefore, I asked my friends to check his identity. Soon they sent me a message that until very, very recently he had worked as the personal driver of a high-ranking official at the Ministry of Justice – the Ministry that supervised all prisons in the country. I continued talking to him, without letting him know what I knew. However, once he started manipulating me towards suicidal stuff, I made the case public, and the administration of the pre-trial detention facility became very embarrassed.

That was in late February or early March. Late at night on the day when this story was published upon my signal, the director removed him from my cell, and said that I could stay alone for as long as I wanted. That was fine with me because I had several lawyers visiting me almost every day, and therefore could bear the overall deficit of socialization.

Being kept alone meant that opportunities for all kinds of nasty psychological or physical operations against me were limited to some extent.

However, that break lasted only four months. In June, after the aforementioned Świtalski-European Parliament-Barroso wave of events, I was moved to another cell, where five other people were held. They were charged with violent and non-violent crimes. I had to adapt to a new situation.

Within the next two months I had to go through several rounds of pressure, such as a totally fake criminal case against my wife, her questioning and intimidation, and daily secret confessions from an emotionally unstable cellmate (charged with violent crime) that the administration had asked him to initiate a quarrel and beat me up 'as a result' of that quarrel.

The purpose was obvious: this was the way high-ranking uniformed people were trying to 'persuade' me to sign a plea for a pardon to the president.

These pressures were accompanied by conversations with the chief detective of the country's prison system. He said he was talking on behalf of the government. One day when the conversation went particularly badly, he directly threatened that I would not survive prison if I did not seek a pardon. I refused, but on the constructive side, counter-proposed withdrawing my application to the European Court in exchange for immediate release and the end of the criminal prosecution. This time he refused.

All this made me only angrier, and in an open letter to José Manuel Barroso, president of the European Commission, I provided names of officials who I believed should be internationally sanctioned for my politically motivated prosecution:

> 'Dear Mr Barroso,
>
> 'Tomorrow on 31 July, exactly 40 days will pass since your "personal" acknowledgement of Azerbaijani ruler Ilham Aliyev as someone still committed to democratic values.
>
> 'Although your statement was in sharp contrast with the resolution on my case adopted by the European Parliament only a week before it, we all recognize that appeasement of dictators sometimes works, and therefore waited for results.
>
> 'However, I am still behind bars – like many other democrats arrested during the current election year. Some of them were arrested even after your testimonial, and hence, at times it becomes difficult to establish the true sequence of events – as to whether your appreciation of Mr Aliyev had occurred one week after the European Parliament's resolution or one week

before the EU-sponsored major gas agreement with him.

'I hereby call on you to resolve the confusion by 1) speedy withdrawal of your futile praise; and 2) urging the European Council to implement the Paragraph 16 of another resolution on the human rights situation in Azerbaijan, which was adopted by the European Parliament last year on 23 May 2012, and had called "to consider the possibility of targeted sanctions against those responsible for human rights violations, should these persist".

'Attached to this letter is the list of judges and prosecution officers directly involved in my case, and thus deserving the "targeted sanction".

'Sincerely,
'Ilgar Mammadov
'Chairman
'Republican Alternative (REAL) Movement
'Azerbaijan'

BUSY SEPTEMBER

Neither the government pressure on me worked, nor my call for international sanctions. Soon I was fully absorbed analysing the 26 thick tomes of the 'findings' of the investigation.

My lawyers did not read it attentively. I noticed that once again their attention was solely on procedural matters. Unlike what we see in detective stories or films, they did not want to engage in analysing factual circumstances. In a way, it made sense as they were copying the most common approach of the European Court of Human Rights, which very rarely went after alleged facts, and concentrated on procedural violations. 'Then what is the point of digging into the quality of evidence?' I heard the lawyers say.

I had time and a very strong motivation to play the role of a chief sleuth, with no regard to what everybody else was thinking or knew. So, I scrutinized every fact, every sentence, and found not just inconsistencies in the line of argumentation of the prosecution, but also strong material proof of my innocence. This became very helpful at the trial, and then, surprise, surprise, priceless at the European Court of Human Rights. In 2017, when reviewing my second application – not about the pre-trial detention, but about the essence of the criminal case, the Court took a very rare path of looking at the trustworthiness of the alleged factual circumstances, and referred to most of my findings.

In September 2013 that was still a long way off. While I was busy reading the multi-volume rubbish of the prosecutors, the Republican Alternative was collecting the 40,000 signatures required for my nomination as a candidate in the presidential elections of 9 October. The task was accomplished within a heroic nine days, whereas the law gave us about 40. The problem was bad legal advice. I had no opportunity to look into the technical aspects of the nomination procedure, while my lawyer and member of the Board of the REAL Movement, Khalid Bagirov, believed that the administration of the jail was preventing the exercise of my right. Given the total injustice surrounding my case, believing in this was easier than reading attentively the complicated text of the Election Code. Inertia in lawyers' thinking was a tremendous phenomenon. I was discovering more and more of it. Finally, a western diplomat, apparently informed by routine communication with the authorities, almost shouted the solution at my people at a round table discussing election matters. Only after that did Khalid realize that we were not utilizing all of the opportunities given by law for my nomination. To his credit, he personally became one of the largest contributors of signatures to the required list by mobilizing quite a big crowd of people around him.

I presume the diplomat was angrier not at our legal team, but at the hopeless coalition of opposition parties and figures which refused to use the last political chance for my release. The coalition was initially planning to nominate a well-known film director, Rustam Ibragimbekov, as its presidential candidate. His chief legal counsel was my lawyer Fuad Aghayev. Mr Ibragimbekov had Russian citizenship, which he had to drop before his nomination. The legal complexity of such cancellation was not properly understood by the coalition. When they realized that his candidacy was a non-starter, time was too short to pick a candidate who could potentially beat the incumbent. So, when the coalition was discussing whom to nominate instead of Mr Ibragimbekov, some of its members argued that I could be the candidate: even if I did not win the election, at least the fact that the main opposition contender was in jail could force the president to release him. However, the coalition refused, and instead nominated a professor who had zero chance of winning.

The diplomats stationed in Baku were aware of the story – both of the underlying quality of legal thinking, and of the intensity of the coalition's dislike of me – and therefore, when confronted with the weak legal advice of my own team too, some of them were understandably upset.

In the end, the Central Election Commission found 'errors' in several thousand of our signatures, and disqualified me from the ballot. We challenged this in the Supreme Court, but once the court had also refused to reverse the decision, I had no option other than calling on my supporters to vote for the registered candidate of the coalition. Which I did, in despair. The whole story of the coalition's refusal to support my candidacy became known to me only after release.

GANJA, THE EUROPEAN YOUTH CAPITAL

The next two months after the elections I spent alone in a very cold and rat-infested cell of the Ganja pre-trial detention facility. My trial was set to be conducted in Sheki, but the newly built Sheki facility was not yet ready to accept inmates. We, more than a dozen people charged in the same criminal case, travelled back and forth between Ganja and Sheki for the court sessions up until 24 December, when we became the first inmates of the Sheki jail.

Due to acute back pain, I was sometimes taken separately, in a jeep rather than the usual old truck. That alleviated the pain a little, but it was still torture due to the road bumps. I had heard a Stalin-era prison anecdote on this situation a little earlier, in the Baku facility. They say Stalin once declared that if you wanted to really torment a prisoner it was enough to constantly take him somewhere rather than keep him in one place. Indeed, every time I had to appeal against another decision of the court in Baku or elsewhere, such as an extension of the detention period, I was terrified by the torturous prospect of being driven to the court and back. Trips in the standard prison truck had been so painful that I always screamed and cursed the entire journey. If people in the nearby cars could hear it, God knows what they thought.

Only in 2024 did I learn that twelve years earlier, back in 2012, my spine had received a hairline fracture when I fell on the stairs near my office. An incompetent doctor had told me everything was fine. He did not notice the fracture. In reality, the pain from compression was unbearable by autumn 2014, when I fell again, on stairs in the Sheki detention facility, but this time on my hands. As a result, the affected spinal bone returned closer to its original position. In 2024, when I showed the CT scan of 2012 to another doctor, he immediately pointed to the fracture. It was the same point where I had the most severe pain for the entire detention time, and beyond.

Health issues were mostly addressed by interventions of the Red Cross, which had been with me from week two of the arrest. It never advertised the practical help its personnel provided, but their contribution to my well-being was essential throughout all the years of privations. The function of the Red Cross was not prevention of the wrongful arrest of politicians ahead of elections or legal facilitation of their release, but what it promised it would do it did with excellence and efficiency.

A former country representative of the Council of Europe in Azerbaijan, Denis Bribosia, sent me some Belgian chocolate. Its expensive quality and appearance provided an artistic contrast with the Ganja prison environment in which I slowly consumed it for weeks. In the same package with the chocolate came a book called *Lord Jim*, written by a Polish-born English writer of the early 20th century, Joseph Conrad. The plot of the novel was built on an act of a young sailor, which could be interpreted as cowardice and therefore did not let him live his entire life with peace of mind. The book further discouraged me from signing any pardon plea to the president, although I do not know if Denis sent it to me with that specific intent or as an allusion to people's various rumoured experiences in the Caspian Sea.

Bribosia's chocolate could only slightly sweeten the November 2013 decision of the Council of Europe to declare Ganja the 2016 European Youth Capital. It was disgusting to hear about that decision while in jail in Ganja, especially because I had spent the last six years as the director of the youth-oriented political activism programme of the Council of Europe. I had to swallow the news somehow with a bigger chunk of the exclusive chocolate.

Ganja beat rival bids from Vilnius, Varna, Galway, La Laguna and Badajoz. A European jury met on 15 November to evaluate the applications. The jury was led by representatives of the Congress of Local and Regional Authorities of the Council of Europe, which from 2014 became an official partner of the European Youth Capital title.

THE TRIAL

The trial started symbolically on 4 November, the 63rd anniversary of the signing of the European Convention on Human Rights.

The court proceedings were a sham. The most significant of the violations are described by the European Court in its second judgment, so I will not elaborate on them here.

The trial was attended by staff from the embassies of several western countries. The United States made a particularly strong effort by being present at each and every hearing in that remote city of Sheki. Deputy head of mission Dereck J. Hogan attended the court several times, but mostly it was Stephen Guice from the public relations department who, for several months, drove for four hours from Baku to Sheki, and then the same distance back.

The judge – no doubt on orders from the political leadership of the country – once attempted to humiliate Mr Hogan by 'attempting' to wake him up, as if he had fallen asleep in the courtroom. The scene was pure stand-up comedy. The purpose was to show to everyone that President Aliyev had a better connection to the US political elite than the State Department, and he did not care about the embassy's opinion. I had worked in the embassy's political-economic section in 2004-2005, so I had a better understanding of what was going on than anybody else in the courtroom.

The Swiss ambassador once attended the trial in person. The German, French, Norwegian, and other embassies sent diplomats to monitor it. All that helped them to produce critical statements once the seven-year prison sentence was pronounced on 17 March. The most critical statement came from the Americans, because they had seen everything, and the government could not accuse them of partial knowledge: 'Our observations lead to the conclusion that the verdicts were not based on the evidence and were politically motivated.'

Because I appealed, the sentence did not become immediately effective. Only after the appellate level could I be transferred to prison. That is why I was held in Sheki till the middle of October 2014.

In May, after I completed another period in solitary, the administration moved me to a cell with five other inmates. Luckily, no provocateurs were among them this time. To enforce the transfer the administration imitated an emergency in the middle of the night by searching my cell for a snake. They said it could penetrate the facility through the sewage system, so they were 'protecting' my life. This was neither the first, nor the last theatrical show, but again, as always, half of me was laughing at it, and the other half was on alert about how nasty things might potentially get.

THE MIME RAPPORTEUR

In the middle of May, the European Court of Human Rights announced that its judgment on my arrest would be made public on 22 May. I asked one of my lawyers, Javad Javadov, to come to Sheki first thing in the morning on that day. As soon as the judgment was on the website, he was to print it out and bring it to me immediately, which he did.

However, a day before that happened, I had two other sudden visitors. Agramunt and Debono Grech came to see me for the second time. The meeting, which I thought would last at least half an hour, was kept as short as ten to fifteen minutes. Pedro Agramunt started the conversation with an irrelevant apology. He said the administration of the penal facility had given them a tour of the prison, thus eating up most of their time, and therefore they had just a few minutes to talk to me before they went back to the helicopter.

Assuming that the co-rapporteurs remembered whom they were meeting and the basic features of my case, I described my situation to the totally oblivious co-rapporteurs. Suddenly Agramunt interrupted me with a question, not even looking at me: 'What have you been arrested for? What is your case about?' For a second or two I was speechless. I looked at Debono Grech, and he shrugged with a guilty smile. I realized that listening to me was not the purpose of the meeting. Somehow, I concluded it in seconds. A quick group photo was taken, and the visitors disappeared.

Neither in the previous year's meetings, nor in this one did I hear Debono Grech's voice. Both times he communicated only by body language. He earned the nickname 'mime rapporteur' from me, but I kept it private. We never met again, and soon he was replaced.

THE ROUTE TWIST EXPLAINED

Two days later I learned from the news that because of Azerbaijan's chairmanship of the Committee of Ministers of the Council of Europe, the Parliamentary Assembly was holding its Standing Committee meeting in Baku. It was attended by senior figures, and included the president of the Assembly, Anne Brasseur, who referred to my case in her introductory speech. According to the evening ANS TV news, the speaker of the Azerbaijani parliament left the event in protest at her speech. I do not know if that was true or not, because the 'we are a sovereign state' bravado has long been typical of the coverage of news about political prisoners.

The accuracy of that record was far less important than Agramunt's intervention at the Standing Committee. While

German MP Frank Schwabe attempted to continue referring to my case, Pedro Agramunt, who took the floor right after him, diverted attention by first implying that he was the most authoritative person in the room as far as my case was concerned because he had met me in jail two days ago, and then drove the discussion in a completely different direction of 'more important' geopolitical topics. The purpose of his abrupt visit to Sheki was now obvious.

GOOD NEWS STIRS MY MEMORY

Having read the European Court's judgment, I became the happiest man on Earth for a few moments. Jubilant, I was sure release and full exoneration were no longer far off because the judgment confirmed the motive of the arrest as political.

An episode from a popular Soviet TV quiz show – 'What? Where? When?' –instantly popped up in my head. In the 1980s or maybe 1990s, one of its non-trivial questions had a hidden snag, which could only be unlocked by understanding the arrest procedure. I remembered neither the question, nor the answer, but the presenter's comment after the quiz in which he explained that if a person in America was arrested in violation of the procedure, then he was subject to immediate release, was firmly imprinted in my memory. The momentous astonishment at the mystery of the relationship between snapshots of a youngster's memory and his destiny was gone as quickly as it came. The lawyer's sceptical eyes on me did not matter either. I had won, and I wanted to celebrate it, at least internally.

ALIYEV IN STRASBOURG

In addition to the PACE Standing Committee meeting in Baku, Azerbaijan's chairmanship of the Council of Europe required someone important from the government to speak at a sitting of the Council's Parliamentary Assembly. President Aliyev went there himself in June 2014 to confront any possible questions from the parliamentarians. Here is how he ordered the Council of Europe to keep quiet, and the Council fell legally silent for the next few years:

> PACE President Anne Brasseur: Thank you very much for your speech, President Aliyev. A number of members want to ask questions. I remind you that you have 30 seconds to ask your questions and not to make statements. We will first have the speakers on behalf of the political groups. The first question is by Mr McNamara on behalf of the Socialist Group.
>
> Mr Michael McNamara: Amnesty International states that there are 19 prisoners of conscience in your jails, President Aliyev. Others say there are more. The European Court of Human Rights has said that the pre-trial detention of one Ilgar Mammadov was unlawful and motivated by electoral considerations. Another, Anar Mammadli, exposed flaws in the recent presidential elections, which you won. Activists of NIDA have been jailed for merely expressing an opinion and calling for peaceful demonstration. This body has adopted a definition of political prisoner, but the rapporteur was denied access to Azerbaijan. Do you believe that that diminishes your legitimacy to chair this body, and will you release those prisoners?
>
> PACE President Anne Brasseur: Thank you. I kindly remind people attending our meeting today – I thank them for coming – not to applaud.

President Ilham Aliyev: First of all, there are no political prisoners in Azerbaijan. All of what Mr McNamara has said is based on false information or his biased approach to our country. Not for the first time, he is trying to insult Azerbaijan, but without any visible success. I am sure that his initiative yesterday will have the same outcome of the initiative of Mr Strasser a couple of years ago, which resulted in the fiasco of January 2013. Unfortunately, Azerbaijan is subject to deliberate provocations. We know the source and we know the reason. It has nothing do with human rights and democracy. It is political. The question Mr Michael McNamara read from his piece of paper was probably given to him by someone who is interested in attacking Azerbaijan.

Mr Michael McNamara: I write my own speeches and questions.

President Ilham Aliyev: I understand. If you want an open discussion, we can find another place for it. There are no political prisoners in Azerbaijan. The report of Mr Strasser failed here in this room because it was based on false information, slander and rumours. Mr McNamara is trying to do the same thing. He is trying to mislead the opinion of the Assembly by repeating that false information. There are no political prisoners. Azerbaijan is a member of the European Court of Human Rights. All issues relating to prisoners can be addressed there. We respect the decisions of the European Court of Human Rights. Therefore, once again, the attempts to attack our country are absolutely groundless. They will have no result.

Unrelated, but the next year McNamara was expelled from his Labour Party of Ireland, and lost his seat in the Parliamentary Assembly as well.

EXHORTATIONS AGAIN

In July, about the time the appellate trial was beginning, the same official who had tried to convince me a year ago to sign a plea for a pardon to the president re-appeared. The previous year his verbal manipulation hooks, designed for very average minds like his own, had included a semi-educated reference to Stalin's daughter Alliluyeva 'who had just died in a care home for elderly people, forgotten by everybody', and a quotation he attributed to a regretful Solzhenitsyn: 'My target was socialism, but I hit Russia.' I was supposed to conclude from the first example that the West's embrace was fleeting, only lasting as long as one was useful, and that the object of the embrace would die forgotten and alone in elderly care. The second example appealed to my patriotism. The tricks were too simple and laughable, but the reality check was imposed by the grimness of the situation: he was a uniformed officer ready to execute the nastiest of orders, and I was in custody.

On the other hand, I felt that this time he was trying to get at least something he could show to his superiors, not necessarily a plea for a pardon. That was a promising development given the European Court's fresh judgment, and it took the edge off the ominous nature of Aliyev's resolute speech in Strasbourg. I repeated to him my position from the previous year – that I was ready to make moves that could help the government save its own face, but I would not ask for a pardon because I had not committed any crime.

When he insisted, I added that even if I wanted to, I could not sign such a plea, because my sentence was not in force yet. How could I inflict on myself the shame of legal illiteracy, after all? In the end, we agreed that I would write a letter to the president calling on him to use his influence to get the local court decision to remand in custody reversed, so that I could attend the appellate court as a free man. That polite, but forceful letter was a huge compromise on my part after such a long time spent in jail for no reason.

He took the letter with him to Baku, and said he would contact me soon. A week or so later I was called to the office of the penal facility chief. He gave me his landline telephone and left the room. The official was on the line. He said with regret that the letter had not worked, because it was 'not sufficient'.

The appellate trial ended on 24 September without any changes in the sentence.

PACE PRESIDENT ADMIRED THE MOUNTAIN VIEW

On that same day, a few hours before the last hearing of the appellate court, Anne Brasseur travelled to Sheki, also by helicopter, like the co-rapporteurs in May. She had promised this meeting with me in her lengthy letter of solidarity earlier in July. The conversation started with me making loud angry remarks to Samad Scyidov, head of the Azerbaijani delegation to PACE, who had accompanied her to the meeting. I was literally shouting at him: 'What are you doing here, when your party men in Parliament accuse me of immorality because of my political activities, and you have never ever raised your voice against them?!'

I do not think Madame Brasseur had ever witnessed such heated inter-party relations in her politically dull Luxembourg. Seyidov pretended he had a call, picked up his cell phone and left the room.

I told Madame Brasseur that the judgment of the European Court was already final on 22 August, and that the authorities were supposed to release me by 22 November, but instead, today I was getting my seven-year sentence confirmed: 'Where are the Council of Europe protections?'

Well, as I learned weeks later, the government had appealed against the European Court's judgment. The appeal failed. That is why the judgment became final not on 22 August, but two months later, on 13 October, and an execution period of three months ending on 13 January 2015 now applied. So, in January I was supposed to be free and acquitted, if the Council of Europe protections, already discredited by my two years behind bars, really worked.

Maybe Madame Brasseur was overwhelmed by the helicopter ride along the Caucasus mountains more than by the prospect of the collapse of the Council of Europe as a serious organization. The only thing I could remember from that meeting was her admiration of the beauty of my country. She sincerely wanted to help, but had absolutely no idea how that could be done.

In the evening of the same day, I was put on a cramped, smoke-filled train and sent back to Baku – this time to prison.

PRISON SCIENCE

Prison life is different from isolation in remand detention due to the higher level of socialization. Now I could spend almost an entire day in the fresh air, play chess, and interact with more than a thousand other convicts. The first question they asked me when I arrived was about my time spent at the remand facility. When they heard it was an unusually long 20 months, they gave a more accurate prediction than any experienced doctor: 'Bro, you gonna get a bad cold very soon. Be ready.'

What these uneducated people understood as a bad cold was in fact a viral infection. People isolated from others for too long become extremely vulnerable to viruses.

Indeed, a month later, a few days after a three-hour conversation with a man in plain clothes who introduced himself as an officer of the Ministry of National Security, I got sick like never before. The guy was probably in charge of the prison, and wanted to make acquaintance with me. From his first and only approach he found out how pointless that was.

His meant-to-be-recruiting talk was mostly about the degradation of the West. After about one hour his mobile phone rang. When he took it out of his jacket pocket, I said, 'Oh, nice iPhone, made in the West.'

'No, no, I swear it's a Chinese replica,' he smirked the way all the Russian-speaking Baku city boys did.

At the end of our second hour, he was telling a story in which he had to drive his car somewhere. I interrupted: 'I can guess it's a German made Mercedes, isn't it?'

'Ha ha.'

After three hours he looked at his watch, signalling the end of the meeting. I asked again: 'That must be Swiss made.'

'Battery operated.'

'Your jacket has a cool western design too, I must say. By the way, what is your name?'

He suddenly realized that the only thing about him that was Azerbaijani at this meeting was his name and surname, and they were most probably fake for the occasion. The rest of him came from the 'damned' West.

The prison's official doctor told one of the inmates, a former medical doctor sentenced for poisoning his personal enemy, to give me a daily injection of antibiotics. As my body temperature did not fall below 39 degrees all week, and as the situation was getting even worse – the injection spot was swollen – I was placed in a medical facility where high-ranking medical professionals of the Penitentiary Service finally took proper care of my health.

DISBARMENT OF MY LAWYER

On 10 December, International Human Rights Day, the Bar Association terminated my lawyer Khalid Bagirov's licence for what he had said at my trial in March. Later on, the local courts rejected his appeal, despite a supporting statement from the PACE President Anne Brasseur.

And what had he actually said? 'Like State, like court ... If there were justice in Azerbaijan, Judge Rashid Huseynov would not deliver unfair and partial judgments, nor would an individual like him be a judge.'

Six years after the incident, the European Court of Human Rights found the disbarment to be in violation of both freedom of speech and freedom to private life.

In December 2022, the Committee of Ministers of the Council of Europe called 'on the authorities to take all necessary steps to ensure that Khalid Bagirov is provided with restitutio in integrum without delay.'

Four years after the Court's judgment, and ten years after the disbarment, Bagirov has still not been reinstated to the Bar, which is one of the key partners of the Council of Europe in Azerbaijan. Maybe he simply does not want to be back in business anymore, having seen the Council of Europe 'protections' at work.

Days before his disbarment, Khalid did me a very great favour. He asked one of his imprisoned clients – a half-Jewish, half-Tatar former Azerbaijani military officer and devout Sunni Muslim (an absolutely uncommon combination), Renat Yusufov, to introduce me to prison life and guide me as much as possible. Renat was an incredible help to me, as I was ignorant of prisoner customs, language, 'etiquette', and risks and opportunities.

COMMITTEE OF MINISTERS JOINS THE RANKS OF THE IGNORED

While I was recovering from the severe infection, in December 2014 the Committee of Ministers of the Council of Europe made its first legal move. Its quarterly Human Rights Meeting called on the authorities to release me 'without delay'.

This was not just a wish, but an action stemming from the key element of the operation of Council of Europe judicial protections. What the European Court issues is basically a declaration. The Committee of Ministers, when it finds it necessary, tells the government how a judgment should be implemented by naming the exact measure to be taken. Measures identified by the Committee of Ministers are either individual or general or both.

Given the 13 January 2015 execution deadline, this first formal action was timely. I had already given up on the political protections of the Council of Europe. If those had not been able to release me for two years already, what was I supposed to expect? Now it was time to focus on legal means.

Maybe to alleviate the pain of the government from this first serious move, early the following week Dragana Filipović, country representative of the Council of Europe in Azerbaijan, loudly praised the 'notable successes achieved in the election system in Azerbaijan' at a public event.

Yet, it did not help. Nothing happened on 13 January. The European Convention on Human Rights was being blatantly violated, the Court was humiliated by a member state, I had been languishing behind bars for two years already, but the Council of Europe would make its next and extremely mild legal move only in a year's time (!), i.e. in December 2015. Until then the Council had more important business to do. I could wait. On 13 January I did not know that yet.

PACE HAS MORE IMPORTANT BUSINESS

As nothing happened on 13 January, the next day I wrote a letter to the Parliamentary Assembly. I argued that as the European Court of Human Rights had established a political motive in my arrest, and as the arrest happened in the context of my nomination for presidential elections, the Assembly should revisit and denounce its positive 2013 presidential election observation report prepared by British MP Robert Walter. I reminded PACE that the conclusions of that mission sharply contrasted with the findings of the long-term, larger, and more professional mission of the OSCE Office for Democratic Institutions and Human Rights.

Zero reaction followed.

In June 2015, I wrote a bitter joke about the communication between Baku and Strasbourg. The Committee of Ministers had asked the government what measures the latter intended to implement to prevent cases like mine. The government replied in writing that it would organize training for judges. That was a hilarious humiliation, but the Council swallowed it, although the Criminal Code of Azerbaijan identified politically motivated court decisions as a crime punishable by imprisonment between five and eight years. So, I wrote a blog post recommending that the Criminal Code be renamed a Training Code, all prisons be closed down, and all criminals taken to classrooms for training.

DIPLOMATIC ROUND CONTINUES

In February 2015, Stavros Lambrinidis, the EU special representative for human rights, visited me. He was accompanied by Malena Mard, the new EU ambassador to Azerbaijan. Today I can recall just one enlightening episode from our conversation. When I referred to the two-year-old Resolution of the European Parliament on my case, he replied with aerobatics worthy of a diplomatic ace: 'Well, you know, Ilgar, nobody "controls" the European Parliament.'

Not without reasons rooted in the rest of our conversation, I understood that episode as a clear message no longer to take seriously anything that came from the club of liberal political experiments called the European Parliament.

I do not remember now if I reminded him of the sarcastic congratulatory letter I had sent to Manuel Barroso in August 2013. The letter said:

> 'Let me congratulate you on the occasion of prolongation of my arrest term by two more months. Two previous prolongations were not sufficient to convince the world in the trustworthiness of your praise of Ilham Aliyev as a committed democrat.
>
> 'I hope that the next prolongation in November will coincide with the third inauguration ceremony for Ilham Aliyev, and you will be able to attend that as well as my court session – both representing the triumph of democracy, freedom, justice, and ... oh, prospective 10% of European gas consumption.
>
> 'The European Parliament's resolution calling for my immediate and unconditional release, the Amnesty International's decision to include my name in the list of prisoners of conscience, and other similar stupidities can wait when you and the Azerbaijan dictator have such a good hydrocarbon "chemistry".'

Six months after my meeting with Stavros Lambrinidis, Malena Mard came alone. That conversation also lasted for an hour or so, but can be summarized in only one phrase, which Ambassador Mard repeated several times for clarity: 'Make your own conclusions.' This was the refrain of a song not promising freedom and victory any time soon.

I do not blame these diplomats at all. I owe them a lot, because, for example, in an emergency between these two meetings I asked a British inmate, who had better access to means of communication, to send an emergency message to Malena Mard. Probably he did, and this helped me overcome that particular emergency. Moreover, the European Union had never given us the promise that the Council of Europe did. This book is about what you can and cannot count upon when a repressive government goes after you with all its might.

EDITOR-IN-PRISON

Navigating the competencies of the Council of Europe was a challenge, but I also had to deal with a lot of incompetencies on the part of the Council people too.

A few months after my meeting with Anne Brasseur, she gave an interview to the online newspaper of her political group – the Alliance of Liberals and Democrats for Europe. An inmate who had access to the Internet noticed the interview just a few hours after publication. I had providently asked him to Google my name from time to time. Part of the interview was about our meeting. It was shocking. Either she or the reporter had chosen an extremely wrong word to describe my fit of rage at Samad Seyidov. The word not only could potentially imply that I was not right, it could also be used against me by the government. This time I was not just angry, but furious, realizing that all these Council of Europe people – however honest, caring and sincere they were – lived in a universe which could decode nothing about the level of sophistication of repressive regimes. I asked the inmate to contact my team immediately, in the middle of the night. Thanks to Piotr Świtalski, by morning the interview had been deleted from the website.

ACTION PLAN 2014-2017

The Council of Europe's country representative Dragana Filipović also visited me several times until she left her post in September 2017. By the time of her departure, half of the budget of the 2014-2017 Action Plan between the Council of Europe and Azerbaijan had been spent on 'the independence and efficiency of the judiciary'.

The cooperation she had established with the government had probably helped me, for example, to be driven to the re-trial in Sheki by car instead of travelling again in that smoky train with security dogs sniffing and barking at me, but I do not think the Council of Europe had been established for such minimalist purposes.

Ambassador Filipović felt freer than other visitors to open up discussion on what had been preventing me from writing a letter to the president. I explained not only to her, but to all of them, that I had no problem writing a polite letter to the president. However, my 2014 letter to him about removal of the court's remand in custody order had shown that what was expected of me was recognition of guilt, that is a plea for a pardon, which I would never make.

Often, I went further, reminding them that I had encouraged other unjustly imprisoned civil society and youth activists to sign such pleas because they were not politicians challenging the president and his party at elections. I had to remind the diplomats of this, because many of them heard from the government that I had a personal emotional – and therefore 'not constructive' – motive in refusing to write to Mr Aliyev.

THE HARDEST LANE IN THE RACE FOR FREEDOM

Indeed, I had chosen the most difficult path of resistance. I could have positioned myself as a civil society activist or human rights defender. In that case there would have been more international support.

For example, in June 2015, the Irish rock band U2 used its concert tour to call for the release of political prisoners in Azerbaijan. Six huge portraits of the recent detainees hung above the stage where U2 performed. Inmates in the prison where I was held had difficulty understanding why my picture was not among them 'if your case is as important as you say it is'. I had been arrested one or two years before these six guys, and had already won my case in the European Court. That's something they achieved later.

I had to explain to everyone that all these six people were human rights defenders or journalists, not politicians. They had not challenged the president. Therefore, it was easier not only for a rock band, but also for other international advocates to call for their release. In my case, the primary expectation was that I should act as a politician – either by mobilizing people to the streets, and escalating the situation up to a revolution if necessary, or by combining a political strategy with a legal one. In other words, I was expected to help myself, because I was a politician and not a human rights defender.

This concert was one of those rare moments when my status as a political contender suited Mr Aliyev. In all other instances the government people went frantic when internationals talked about me as his opponent.

One of the consequences of my choice to fight for my freedom as a politician, and not human rights defender, was that during the entire time in custody and afterwards I was not even nominated for any international awards, unlike some other political prisoners.

Even now, every step I or my family members take in a bank or elsewhere requires lengthy and burdensome declarations on political exposure. Azerbaijan has happily accepted all the Council of Europe standards about political exposure, but the only people whose life is made harder by those standards are the political opponents of the government, and their families. The global actors who have stigmatized the profession of politician around the world wanted various unelected people and institutions to run the global agenda. Ironically, Azerbaijan has become the most successful example of how manipulation with transparency standards can kill democracy in a country. No one wants to be a politician. People with ambition play the part of civil society activists or journalists, receive the prohibited international democracy funding in secret, and thus are only able to change the government if and when strong social protest ripens, not improve its democratic institutions through electoral competition. The net outcome of this vicious circle is that those who stand behind their nominal donors always make deals with the repressive governments on economic benefits for their respective global businesses or countries.

NEW WAVE OF ASSAULTS

While the Council of Europe was contemplating the juicy spittle on the face of its protections after 13 January 2015, the government started losing patience with my refusal to surrender.

Once, I was sitting on my bed in the barracks, and solving chess problems from an old magazine. That was in the middle of May. When I reached the one marked as 'Lenin's favourite', several guards suddenly entered the barracks to search my bed and adjacent small locker. It lasted for ten minutes or so. The guards left without saying anything. Several minutes later I was called to the deputy chief of the prison. He had guilty eyes, and was nervously smoking. Could he be acting? I did not know. Staring at the floor, he declared that I would be placed in the punishment cell.

Formally, I was being disciplined for 'obstructing a routine search'.

Strange enough, they allowed me to take a pen to the punishment cell. In a movie-like episode, lying in bed I drew Lenin's chess problem on the wall, the same size as a regular magazine, and easily solved it. Moreover, they took me for a daily walk for an hour or two. So, except for the solitary confinement cell's terrifying design of a medieval gaol, it was not so much a punishment as a show of desperation, and readiness to escalate tensions if I did not write the plea for a pardon to 'the best shah we have ever had', as the prison chief had put it in one of our conversations.

The next month the administration imposed restrictions on my telephone access. While all other inmates could make phone calls an unlimited number of times for a small bribe, I was limited to the two quarter-hour slots a week envisaged in the law. (Before the restriction, once we were able to plan things in such a way that I called home when Daniel Kaufmann, president of the Revenue Watch Institute, was visiting my wife and daughter. That was useful for my morale because failures of the Council of Europe protections suggested that I should mobilize the international mining sector transparency initiatives, in which I had been an activist.)

The limited access to the telephone was the beginning of a more serious 'step-by-step' plan. Azerbaijani officials are religious about the 'step-by-step'. At planning meetings, they pronounce these words in English, even if they do not speak the language. The concept is present in all their actions, and it mostly works.

In August, when I had already exhausted my weekly telephone call limit, one of the inmates, notorious locally for wearing a metallic pin with Aliyev's portrait on his jacket, approached me from behind and hit me on the neck so hard that I fell. He shouted: 'Is this the scoundrel who goes against our president?'

Then he hit me two more times, before other inmates took him away. In the following days some of them kindly made sure they were always nearby to protect me from further attacks.

The prison administration was rather scared by this reaction from other inmates. Officers feared that one day I could use this level of respect against the administration. Therefore, they took me to the prison's industrial shops several times, where they filmed me carrying scrap metal furniture from one point to another according to their orders. This ridiculous action lasted several minutes, and was meant to document my 'worker' status, thus making it impossible for me to take any position in the criminal hierarchy. As if I had ever aspired to one. All the inmates laughed at this effort when they heard about it.

I described this incident in a public post after my time in prison. Madat Guliyev, who was the head of Azerbaijan's prison network at the time of this performance and was later promoted to become the country's spy chief, had been suddenly removed from his post by the president in 2019 and appointed minister in charge of the military industry. In my scathing article I wrote that it was now his turn to carry scrap metal back and forth, as he had failed in the James Bond role. Guliyev was one of those who coordinated all the nasty pressure against me in detention, but, I guess, without personal enthusiasm, and only as a matter of his perverted understanding of 'duty'.

In mid-September the administration shut off my access to telephone calls completely, and without giving a formal reason. I was supposed to be terrified by what was coming.

And it came. On the evening of Friday 16 October, the prison chief, his deputy and another guard, confident that I would not have access either to a lawyer or telephone before

Monday, beat me up in the chief's office. Maybe they even filmed this – in order to report the operation up to a higher level.

Three days prior to that, on 13 October 2015 – exactly one year after the judgment of the European Court of Human Rights became final – the Supreme Court of Azerbaijan had adopted its long-delayed ruling on my case, upholding the sentence. So, I was supposed to be terrified not only by the beating, but also by the performance manipulating the date: 'Look what we can do to you! We do not give a shit about your European Court!'

Then I was placed in the punishment cell again, the one with Lenin's chess problem, and was told someone from the 'top' would be coming to talk to me. At that point I started shouting all the profanities I had accumulated in my life to describe my opinion of the person who was coming to talk to me, and those who had sent him. I yelled and yelled and didn't stop hitting and kicking the door.

This lasted for half an hour or so. Suddenly, the guards unlocked the door, and escorted me back to the barracks. I was told that the car bringing the official from the top had suddenly returned to Baku city centre because of urgent business. That urgent business happened to be the appointment of Madat Guliyev as the country's chief intelligence official. President Aliyev unexpectedly fired the old one – Eldar Mahmudov, arrested all his friends, and appointed Guliyev to replace him. The co-incidence probably saved me from a conversation, which this time might have been extremely destructive.

That was a pure miracle. On the not so bright side, the next week my teeth prosthesis collapsed as a result of the beating. The entire upper right side was gone, and I could not have the teeth replaced until after my release. I did not lose my smile, but it took me some time to lose the habit of covering my mouth with my hand.

ARTICLE 52

In December, two months after the beating and 11 months past the deadline for execution of the judgment, Thorbjørn Jagland, secretary general of the Council of Europe, launched an inquiry under Article 52 of the European Convention on Human Rights to find out how domestic law in Azerbaijan made sure that the Convention was properly implemented. This was his second legal move in almost three years since the arrest. The previous one had been his request to the Court in April 2013 to make reviewing my case a priority.

This second initiative helped me only to get some unreliable verbal guarantees from the government that there would be no more physical violence. But before I heard that unconvincing promise, I had to go through another unproductive conversation.

A GENERAL THIS TIME

The year 2016 started with one of the top managers of the prison system, with the rank of general, coming to test anew the possibility of me signing a plea for a pardon. We, or rather mostly he, talked for three hours. He told me stories from his long experience in law-enforcement, trying to assure me – as if I was in a debate on the matter – that President Aliyev was in favour of close ties with the West and Turkey. He used to be a criminal investigator in the mid-1990s, interrogating the detained Turkish agent who had led an attempted coup d'état. He believed he had convinced the guy that Aliyev Senior was in favour of a strong alliance with the West as opposed to an alliance with Russia. I listened, but not to his stories though – rather to what his efforts might mean for me safety-wise once he heard me say 'No' yet again.

In the end, as we both stood up and were in the doorway, I decided to ask him directly so that he understood his responsibility if anything happened: 'Now that I've said "No" again, should I expect a repetition of what happened here in October?'

'No, don't worry at all. I give my word. Nobody here in prison will lay a finger on you ever again.'

He kept his word. Later on, I learned that he was either a relative or somehow otherwise close to the deputy chief of the prison, who had been a most enthusiastic participant in my beating.

POST-PREVENTION OF TORTURE

A month or two later, in March or April, I described all the incidents of mistreatment in prison to visitors from the Committee for the Prevention of Torture, which is the anti-torture body of the Council of Europe. Its group members did not give me any business cards, nor did they all give their names. They said their team had been inspecting the detention facilities of Azerbaijan for one week, and included various experts, even a psychiatrist so that inmates could use his advice if they had issues to be reported. I had none, but I described to them not only the incidents, but also the political context of the case.

After our long conversation, as I was walking the group towards the exit, the psychiatrist looked angry, and whispered: 'Believe me, Europeans can do nothing. You can only be released with forceful American pressure.' I asked him why Americans would bother doing that. His reply was as politically naïve as it was sincere, and was 'illustrated' with his clenched fist: 'To demonstrate their power, to show that they can do it.'

More entertaining and uplifting was the reaction of the French or francophone lady in the group to my description of one of the assaults on me. Generally, she could not hide her relief at finding me mentally stable. Probably, one of the strategies of the government was to persuade the internationals that Ilgar was out of his mind.

So, I told the visitors what had happened shortly before the October beating. One of the inmates, a friend of the August attacker, came to my barracks and asked me to go with him 'for a serious talk man-to-man'. That was a scary sign, because he was a very sick heroin addict. Unlike normal fights, when an inmate called someone to a relatively hidden place so that nobody would see what was happening, this guy called me to the soccer pitch, which was fully under surveillance cameras. I was sure he did that on orders from the prison administration in order to document my likely physical retaliation, and then present an abridged video clip of it as an unprovoked attack.

I continued: 'We arrived at the small soccer pitch, and I immediately folded my arms across my chest so that I did not look like an attacker on camera, and kept more than one metre away from him…'

'Oh, a politician working for the camera, I can see that,' she said with friendly irony, adding positive vibes to the atmosphere of the conversation.

When they heard the whole story, not just the preface, I am sure all of them had a much better understanding of the risks of our profession. The guy cut a vein, tried to throw the blood into my face, and shouted that he was going to cut my body with the same razor blade – now or when I was asleep – so that I would get infected with the HIV and other deadly infections he carried. Other inmates quickly took him away.

Months later, he voluntarily moved to the barracks for gays. Living in that barracks was perceived by the other prisoners as the highest level of humiliation, not least because its residents were forced to do all the dirty cleaning work in the prison. Apparently, the prison administration knew his 'secret', and had terrorized him into doing such nasty things as the attack on me, but at some point, he felt prouder moving to that 'ignoble' barracks than following the dirtiest illegal orders from senior prison officers.

His friend, the August attacker, approached me again two years later, when he was terminally ill, and at the very point where he had attacked me asked for forgiveness. I could not say 'No'.

AGRAMUNT FOR THE LAST TIME

A month before the Committee for the Prevention of Torture, Pedro Agramunt visited me for the third time, now in his capacity as president of the Parliamentary Assembly of the Council of Europe. He became a completely different person! He wasn't in a hurry and listened well to everything I said. The British national who was accompanying him from the Secretariat took our photo at his initiative. After an hour I asked him how much time we had. He said in a very relaxed way: 'As much as you need.'

That was good, but the most impressive remark came at the end. We had all suspected him of being the most notorious figure in Azerbaijan's infamous 'caviar diplomacy' – the policy of bribing Council of Europe officials en masse – and that suspicion had explained his behaviour at the first two meetings. At this meeting though, he encouraged me to stay strong and not to surrender. And he looked totally honest.

To no avail. Anyway, next year he was removed from office only six months before the end of his final term, due to the disarray of his visit to Syria.

PACE elected its fourth president to see me in prison in blatant violation of the Convention. In total, I counted six of them from behind bars. Six PACE presidents per criminal sentence was really too much. Here is what I wrote on my blog in May 2013 about the first one, Jean-Claude Mignon:

'Whose Council of Europe is This?!

'I am deeply disappointed, to say the least, by the handling of the issue of my current continued arrest at the meeting between Mr Jean-Claude Mignon, President of the PACE, and Azerbaijan's ruler Ilham Aliyev on 26 May. The latter has arrested me under fabricated charges nine month to the presidential elections of 16 October 2013 in order to impede my nomination and secure comfortable fraud. From what Mr Mignon has told to my colleagues after the meeting, we derive that he had submissively accepted Mr Aliyev's hint about possibility of resolving my case by January 2014, i.e. after the accomplishment of all the fraud plans.

'Now I can see even better as to why at the 23 January 2013 PACE session – which has given a carte blanche to Mr Aliyev for renewed repressions – Mr Samad Seyidov, head of Azerbaijani delegation at PACE, famously exclaimed: "This is not your Council of Europe! This is my Council of Europe!"

'In the past 13 years of Azerbaijan's membership, there has always been a "greater than democratic political wisdom" in the process that has shaped the CoE-Azerbaijan relations. As a result, Azerbaijan has degraded from its poor pre-accession democracy to the current Middle Eastern despotism.

'My call for action has been ignored by the April 2013 session of PACE. Now I call on the July 2013 session: please suspend the voting rights of Azerbaijani delegation if Mr Aliyev does not stop treating his election opponents this way. Whose Council of Europe is this?!

'P.S. Mr Mignon, the next day after your meeting with Aliyev, his "court" rejected my appellation, and thus made final the decision on prolongation of my arrest by three more months."

REFUSING TO EMIGRATE: EXECUTE THAT DAMNED JUDGMENT

I cannot remember now, but I believe it was the first half of 2016, and then the beginning of 2017 and 2018 when a non-EU member European country, verbally, via trusted friends, offered me full and immediate immigration – right from prison to the plane and so on. All three times I refused. To our understanding, those offers had been made in coordination with the government. I had become a real headache for multi-billion European projects with Azerbaijan. All three times I insisted that the judgment of the Court must be executed. I was too old to emigrate in such a situation.

SIDELINE THE CONVENTION

In the meantime, the government threatened to amend the Constitution so that it could refrain from executing the European Court's judgments whenever it wanted. Guess who was appointed to nominally author the amendment? You'll remember him from the beginning of this book – Rafael Jabrayilov.

In early April, Stefan Schennach, then newly elected co-rapporteur of the Parliamentary Assembly, 'expressed his concerns regarding a parliamentary initiative that would impede the unconditional implementation of decisions of the European Court of Human Rights, which is a binding obligation on all members of the Council of Europe'.

In the end, the initiative did not get far, but maybe that was not even the intention. What if the appointment of Jabrayilov was meant to make circumstances look terrifying to me personally? Even if it was not, I must admit that the wide range of emotions and perseverance the government had put to use in order to frighten me had shown that its desire to keep me imprisoned outweighed the Council of Europe's aspiration to secure my release.

ACTION MOVIE FEATURING A UN MISSION

In May, while I was returning to the Baku prison from another futile re-trial in Sheki, I had another strange experience. Having collected inmates from the railway wagon, the truck took us to different prisons. I was the last. I was driven to the gates of the prison. I could see it from the very small window, no bigger than the palm of a hand. Then the truck waited for several minutes and suddenly departed at huge speed.

I could not understand what direction we were going in. After a while the truck stopped in the middle of a busy suburban street. It was encircled by dozens of guards. The door opened, I was quickly moved to another truck, and it instantaneously took off at a crazy speed.

I had no idea where they were taking me and why. It was just another of the many scenes where I lived as if in an action movie. In about half an hour or so we arrived at the pre-trial detention facility. I was met there personally by its chief who knew me from 2013. He was unusually friendly, playing the role of a hotel manager rather than a prison chief.

To a certain extent, he had my trust. In 2013, he had given me a hint that his high-ranking colleague, who had been trying to drag me into signing a plea for a pardon, was talking baloney about the immediate effect of a signature. As if I was going to sign it! The limit to my trust though was set by a confession of my emotionally unstable cellmate who had been told to harass me around the same time in summer 2013. According to him, this chief had personally instructed him to hit me with his sportsman's fist, which he never did.

Actually, he was not the only officer to behave so controversially. Some 'confided' in me on different occasions over the years, stating things like, 'Had you signed it, I would have lost respect for you,' or 'You would be dead by now if you did not expose the pressures we put you under here' etcetera. The confusing side of such outbursts of frankness is that you never know how to read them. Is it his real opinion or it is just an attempt to build trust and personal bonds for his future operational needs? So, you cannot act on this knowledge. You may only choose to believe that it was a rush of sincerity. In that case you could motivate yourself for further struggle. Resources for motivation were scarce anyway, and this mental exercise was handy at times.

So, I was trying to figure out what was going on. The prison chief called the duty officer via the public address system and instructed him to give me the best 'room', to provide me with fruit, food and drink, and to make sure that the TV set and radio were working in that 'room'.

Then he turned to me with the intentionally fake grimace of a cheap roadside motel owner. His hand gestures repeated the feminine curve of a classic Azerbaijani tea glass: 'Can we serve you something special?'

We laughed together at my obviously negative answer, which I nevertheless found necessary to say.

This spectacle did not last long. On the way to the cell, the guards were stopped by a walkie-talkie call, and took me not to the cell, but to another truck, which quickly delivered me back to the prison.

The first thing I learned from the excited inmates back 'home' was that a foreign delegation had been walking around the prison barracks, asking people if they had seen me around. The prison system was hiding me from international visitors.

The next day, the same group came to the prison again, and this time we talked. They happened to be from the UN Working Group on Arbitrary Detention.

I am still not sure if the entire dramatic performance of the previous day had the purpose of disarming my critical thinking ability by boosting my ego ahead of the meeting with this group. Maybe I am overthinking it, but look at what our conversation was about.

The group was part of the UN Human Rights Council, and it asked me if I wanted my case to be taken for consideration by the Council.

I answered with a sober 'No'. I knew from my conversations with lawyer Fuad Aghayev that the European Court of Human Rights would refuse to issue a judgment on any case if in parallel it had been sent to the UN Human Rights Council. My second application to the ECHR – on the merits of the sentence – was already in Strasbourg. A favourable ruling from the Court would greatly reward and bolster my efforts towards enforcement of the initial judgment. Therefore, I had no interest in undermining the process by diverting attention to the UN body.

THE ECONOMISTS

While the UN group was still in Baku, *The Economist* magazine published an article about Azerbaijan, in which it viewed our country's prospects through the prism of two opposites – the Pashayevs, the family of the first lady, and our Republican Alternative movement. Rebecca Vincent, human rights activist blacklisted by the government of Azerbaijan, was able to smuggle the magazine to me with her 'Stay strong!' handwriting on it.

This reminded me of a comic episode of 2013, during my early days in jail, when guards had confiscated several issues of the magazine sent to me by friends. An officer from the Ministry of National Security with an intimidating posture and people from the administration of the detention facility brought me to an interrogation, which lasted only a minute:

'What's your name?'

'What's your name, officer? You introduce yourself first.'

'What's your interest in this magazine? Why do you read the press in English?'

'It's my favourite. I've been reading it for a long time.'

'What do you want to find there? What does it write about?'

'Officer, if you don't give it to me now, the next issue will write about you.'

The interrogation ended at this very point, and I immediately received the magazine package. However, only now, while checking online resources for this book, did I learn that they had confiscated one issue – from 22 March 2013, which actually mentioned my case in an article called 'Azerbaijan and the Council of Europe'.

Now, three years later in 2016, I was reading exactly what I wanted to read in the magazine. Except, knowing how vindictive such political regimes are, I regretted that the comparison of our movement and the ruling clan quoted Natig Jafarli, executive secretary of REAL and a prominent economist. Three months after the publication, he was arrested too: as the European Court of Human Rights found four years later, the arrest had also been politically motivated under Article 18 of the Convention.

Fortunately, his ordeal lasted for only about a month, and he was promptly set free. Natig had already been successful at the European Court before – for violation of his rights as a candidate in parliamentary elections. This Article 18 judgment became final two days before the 9 February 2020 elections, which were also stolen from him. Currently, his application is still pending at the Court. The efficiency of the Council of Europe protections is self-evident: none of the politically sensitive judgments translate into lasting improvements in the judicial and legal systems, let alone in the electoral system.

A few days after Natig's release I was visited by another UN official, Michel Forst, special rapporteur on the situation of human rights defenders. Later, he wrote this in his mission statement:

> 'Human rights defenders see the European Court of Human Rights as the ultimate arbitrator on their appeals, when they are rejected in the domestic courts. However, the rulings of the European Court of Human Rights are not executed by the Government in cases related to human rights defenders (for example, Ilgar Mammadov), despite numerous calls from the Committee of Ministers of the Council of Europe.'

I do not think anybody at the Council of Europe read his report in autumn 2016. The Council at the time was that very figurative ostrich with its head buried in the sand.

As stated earlier in this book, having foreseen the likely poor effectiveness or total failure of the Council of Europe protections, I was building a parallel line of defence. I wanted to put into use my membership of the Advisory Board of the Revenue Watch Institute to make my incarceration as economically costly for the government as possible.

Azerbaijan had been going through regular validation of its performance at the Extractive Industry Transparency Initiative (EITI) – a global partnership of governments and civil society. The Revenue Watch Institute was the most important international civil society player within the Initiative.

I knew that our government had an even stronger voice inside the 'independent' civil society of Azerbaijan than inside the Council of Europe. Therefore, I asked some trusted people to bring me the material that the next EITI Board meeting would be looking at. They somehow managed to sneak those preparatory papers into the prison. Having read them, and enraged at the Azerbaijani civil society contributors who had obviously done everything possible to keep my name out of the process, I wrote the following letter to the Board:

'Dear Members of the EITI Board,

'I have read with great interest the 31 August 2016 Report on initial data collection and stakeholder consultation by the EITI International Secretariat.

'As someone who had served in 2007-2013 (till the date of arrest on 4 February 2013) as an Advisory Board Member of the Revenue Watch Institute, I found it quite surprising that the report has no mention of my case – at least at the first 97 pages, which were available to me.

'Let me remind to the Secretariat some key aspect of the case, before I conclude by analysing the significance of validation of the Azerbaijan report in current circumstances.

'1. The European Court of Human Rights has established that my arrest and continued detention have been not only illegal, but also politically motivated: 'silence him for criticizing the government'.

'2. The US Embassy in Baku, which had made huge efforts to monitor each of the 25-30 sessions of my trial in a remote town, has also concluded that the verdict was not based on evidence and was politically motivated.

'3. European Parliament adopted in 2013 a separate resolution with my name in its title calling for my immediate and unconditional release.

'4. Committee of Ministers of the Council of Europe adopted 8 documents insisting on my immediate release in line with the above judgment of the European Court.

'This is not the full list of key facts of the case. The EITI could have been more attentive to its strong legal base, especially as it concerns someone who had been a long time partner and activist of the Initiative.

'Today Azerbaijan is short of cash for the construction of critically important gas export pipelines. International Financial Institutions have included Azerbaijan's EITI compliance into main criteria for loan eligibility. Approval of the loans are expected to happen mostly in the end of this year – after the 35th (?) Board meeting of the EITI.

'In this regard, the next validation is becoming a rare and unique tool capable of ensuring release of those political prisoners who had worked together with you on transparency and accountability in the extractive industry.

'I understand that the EITI is under heavy pressure from the energy companies willing to secure the gas pipelines. Geopolitics can stop countries and inter-governmental organizations, but not civil society actors. Although I, and other political prisoners fully support the idea of South Gas Corridor to Europe, we believe that the civil society institutions should not make any compromise to the geopolitical goals at the expense of transparency champions.

'Sincerely yours,
'Ilgar Mammadov'

Once the letter reached the Board, my suspicion that Azerbaijani civil society leaders were involved in this whitewash operation only grew stronger. One of them openly stated discontent to my confidants: 'Why did you take the report to Ilgar? Now the government will think I was involved in that.'

The Board review in October 2016 was negative for the government. In March of the next year, Azerbaijan was forced to leave the EITI at enormous material and moral cost to its energy projects.

ENTERTAINING MYSELF WITH LITERARY STYLE

By the time of Natig Jafarli's release I was so fed up with the years of procrastination at the Committee of Ministers that I added a comparative chapter to my reply to Svetlana Alexievich, Belarusian winner of the Nobel prize in literature, who earlier had sent me her famous book with her supportive inscription on it. Here is what I wrote in Alexievich's native Russian, imitating her own style:

> 'In 1984, a gas leak blew up an apartment block in a residential area of Baku. Fifty-nine people died. Prosecutors quickly "found" the culprit. It turned out to be an ethnic Armenian Serge Haykazyan, an engineer at the gas distribution network. The case acquired a political flavour, as society in those years vividly, albeit in whispers, discussed the terrorists who pretended to be speaking on behalf of or in the name of the Armenian people: an explosion in the Moscow metro, a very recent explosion on a Baku bus, an explosion at Paris airport, etc.
>
> "However, all courts of the Azerbaijan Soviet Socialist Republic, including the Plenum of the Supreme Court of the Republic, fully acquitted Haykazyan. Then the Azerbaijani prosecutors laid the groundwork for the Central Office of the USSR Prosecutor General itself to challenge the court decision. And it did so. However, in 1988, despite such

powerful pressure, the Supreme Court of the same Azerbaijan SSR acquitted Haykazyan for the fourth time.

'It is important to note that all these years the suspect remained free and not behind bars.

'Today, Azerbaijan is a member of the UN, the OSCE, the Council of Europe and others. The European Court in Strasbourg decided that my arrest was politically motivated. The Committee of Ministers of the Council of Europe has adopted eight documents insisting on my release. PACE, the European Parliament and the UN Human Rights Council have declared me a political prisoner and demanded my release. And I have already spent more time behind bars than Haykazyan was tried in Soviet Azerbaijani courts. So, what conclusions should people draw?'

LAYERS OF PROCRASTINATION

Procrastination at the Committee of Ministers continued for a full three years after the deadline for execution of the judgment. Prior to that, we had lived through two years of procrastination by PACE.

Business psychology experts now say that people may procrastinate even without knowing it. That applies to individuals though. It is impossible for a huge organization with so many affiliated structures, bosses and experts not to understand what was going on. Maybe after this book somebody will seek, in the first place, and find a clear answer as to why the procrastination was happening all those years.

The government had been telling the Committee that the European Court's 22 May 2014 judgment was only about my pre-trial detention, and not about the sentence. This legal-looking absurd argument referred to the fact of conviction, which was the result of 'fair review' at the local court, 'not yet assessed by the European Court'.

Any political body acting in a timely fashion and with self-respect would immediately shut down such a conversation, because its obvious goal was procrastination. Nevertheless, only three (!) years past the deadline (!), in December 2017, the highest body of the Council of Europe sued the government at the Grand Chamber of the European Court as a non-compliant member under Article 46 § 4 of the European Convention on Human Rights. I had been bombarding it incessantly for years with requests to do that immediately. Here is the final section of a desperate letter the Committee received from me six months prior to this momentous event:

> 'The conclusions below are based on the facts and thoughts reflected in all my letters to the Committee of Ministers and the Council of Europe officials in the past four-and-a-half years, i.e. not only on this one.
>
> '1. The authorities will continue attempting new provocations against me, my family, and my supporters every time when the Committee of Ministers postpones punitive action against them for another three months period.
>
> '2. In fact, the 11 quarterly postponements by the Committee of Ministers since December 2014 the authorities do perceive as an invitation to exert such a pressure on me which, they believe, would demoralize me into surrender and thus take the burden of the case off the Council of Europe shoulders.
>
> '3. I will not surrender, even if some people at the Council of Europe really wanted that to happen.
>
> '4. The Council of Europe will suffer a serious reputational blow if am not released before 4 October

2017 (i.e. before the two-thirds of my sentence which entitle me to an actual release on probation anyway), because the Council's protections against politically motivated imprisonment will prove to be dysfunctional.

'5. My release any time after the 4th of October will make crucially important a fundamental redesign of the Council of Europe protections – at the level of the Convention, of organizational structure, and of personnel.'

So, what had the Committee of Ministers been waiting for? To answer that question, we need to go back to the Article 52 inquiry by the secretary general. I wrote earlier in this book that the inquiry had been made in December 2015, almost a year past the deadline for execution of the judgment.

One extra year of empty talk, and in January 2017, six months before his retirement, Philippe Boillat, the Council of Europe's director general of human rights and rule of law, came to Baku to finalize discussions on what could be done. Admittedly, he was the most influential person within the Council's bureaucracy after the secretary general.

He totally failed in the talks. The government convinced him that the president would soon introduce a package of legislative amendments, which would make me a free man. And he happily left Azerbaijan for retirement. Recently, I found his last speech in the Council, made on 1 June 2017 during a debate on the annual report on execution of the Court judgments. Available on the Council's website it was absolutely out of touch with reality.

The government was working and not only through him. In February, Alain Destexhe, another PACE co-rapporteur, visited me right after his one-to-one meeting with President Aliyev. As I was trying to explain how the Article 52 team had been fooled by the government, he said this, literally: 'I do not have keys of this place to take you out of here.' I was sure this phrase had been put in his mouth by the government as a psychological manipulation tool, to trick me into desperation and submission. As a result, I became even more resolute. Later on, Mr Destexhe had to resign as one of the notable figures in the caviar diplomacy scandal.

Angry at the Committee of Ministers, following its June 2017 decision I wrote this on my blog:

> 'On 8 June the Committee of Ministers laughed at me again by noting in its 11th (!) quarterly decision a 'positive development' in my case. Mr Aliyev joined the laughter by submitting a draft law (which the Committee of Ministers scleroticly believes would release me) on the last day of the supplementary session of parliament. Now the parliament will assemble for plenaries again only in October-December, i.e. after the 12th quarterly tickling by the Committee of Ministers Human Rights Meeting in September. I am afraid they will tickle each other to death of laughter by the end of my prison sentence.'

The package Mr Boillat and the Committee of Ministers had been counting upon was adopted by the parliament ten (!) months after the former's visit, that is in October. As expected, the Council of Europe was completely fooled. The legislative change which was supposed to result in my release required a letter of admittance of guilt – so that I could ask for a parole or probation release. I had been warning everyone for years that this was not acceptable.

Decisions of the Committee of Ministers on the execution of judgments are typically published one day after the quarterly meeting. The last quarterly of 2017 ended on 7 December. None of us was aware yet of the Committee's decision to initiate the infringement procedure against

Azerbaijan in accordance with Article 46 § 4 of the Convention.

In this situation, the government attempted to use the microscopic time gap between the decision and its publication to get a word from me that I would request early parole. Yes, they were that petty, and clung to the smallest opportunity, because they knew what they wanted.

On 7 December Prime Minister Novruz Mammadov issued a statement practically offering me parole. I am sure that if I had said 'yes', the government would have convinced the Committee of Ministers to refrain from using this 'nuclear option which has never been intended for use'. Maybe we would never be able to see the decision published. The Committee meetings were not public, and any gentleman's agreements were possible there.

I asked my lawyer Fuad Aghayev to immediately respond to the offer on my behalf by rejecting it outright. Around the same dates I formally cancelled contracts with my two other trusted lawyers because I knew that the government might harass them into writing a conditional release plea on my behalf. To safeguard them from this highly likely pressure, I asked Fuad to announce that Shahla Humbatova and Javad Javadov had been dismissed as my lawyers. Not that these two lawyers had less integrity or fortitude. I just wanted to curb the risks.

After that, the Committee of Ministers' resolution on initiation of the procedure was published, and in a few days Fuad somehow managed to bring me the text of it, thus breaking another round of blockade – from time to time the prison administration banned lawyers from bringing me any 'unrelated' documents.

In the meantime, as the risk was gone, I resumed my contracts with Shahla Humbatova and Javad Javadov. They had both been of immense support to me during the toughest times.

Draft resolutions of the Committee of Ministers put to the vote must be supported by two-thirds of the 47 country representatives in Strasbourg in order to pass. The vote is open to the participants, but confidential for the general public. Yet, my trusted people somehow learned who was voting and how in December 2017: Azerbaijan and Turkey voted against, while Russia, Ukraine, Georgia, Moldova, Serbia, and an unnamed western European country abstained, which equalled to voting against the initiation of the infringement procedure. I cannot guarantee the accuracy of this information, but it looks credible.

2018 BEGINS

The eight months following the initiation of the infringement procedure I also spent behind bars, waiting for the Grand Chamber response to that simple question lying at the heart of the infringement procedure: 'By refusing to exonerate Ilgar Mammadov is Azerbaijan compliant with its membership obligations or not?'

I practically had no foreign guests visiting me at the time. Suddenly in April, Norica Nicolai, the European Parliament's permanent rapporteur for Azerbaijan, showed up. She was a no name for me. I only saw her meeting President Aliyev one day before. 'Not a promising sign,' I thought, given the experience with Caesar Preda (see below), and Alain Destexhe. I kept our meeting very official. She looked a bit lost as to what she was doing there. Only after my release did I learn from a very honest European representative that she had been sent to see me by the Azerbaijani government because Brussels was requesting another meeting for 'a very important delegation'. By sending Nicolai, the government gained ground to decline that request: 'It was enough for Ilgar to have one EU visitor at a time. Another one in a very short time would mean too much attention, and is not acceptable.

He is just an ordinary criminal.' Thus, the government skilfully played not only European institutions against each other, but even led people within the same institutions into obstructing each other's work.

CONDITIONAL FREEDOM

On 13 August the Appellate Court in Sheki issued a surprise decision to grant me conditional release. As part of the conditions, I was required to check in at the Probation Office every ten days. Additionally, I was prohibited from travelling abroad, running for office in elections, and more.

Looking back at the time in detention, I spent 20 months in pre-trial, that is, in a remand facility, and 46 months in prison. In our Soviet past, time in a remand facility was considered to be more of a hardship to a human being than time in prison. Therefore, every day in a remand facility was deemed equivalent to a day and a half in prison. As I heard from a British inmate, similar coefficients exist in his homeland and some other European countries. By calculating my time behind bars that way, it can be argued that the Council of Europe protections reduced my seven-year sentence only by eight months.

Even if we do not apply such coefficients, the reduction was only by 18 months. Is this outcome adequate to the declared credentials of the Council as a champion of human rights and the rule of law?

Another ridiculous aspect of the conditional release was that the local court formally extended the punishment sentence from the original seven years to seven and a half years and ten days. This was, to put it mildly, very far from the notion of execution of the European Court's judgment. The government could not stop laughing at the Council even when they released me.

Other explicit and implicit conditions were to be followed. I was supposed to: abstain from running in elections till almost 2027; prove by my behaviour that I had been 'corrected'; never change my residential address without informing the probation agency; make a timely appearance before probation officers in response to their calls; sign a special register every ten days at the probation agency; and not travel abroad.

Yet, I was happy because I could fight all these limitations from home, and not from behind bars.

ACKNOWLEDGEMENTS

Not allowed to travel abroad in the first eight months after release, I was very glad finally to have a beer in a Baku restaurant with Stefan Schennach, member of the Austrian parliament and PACE co-rapporteur on Azerbaijan.

Our first meeting in 2017 was a bit scandalous, although the incident did not leak into the press. His company was another PACE co-rapporteur Cezar Florin Preda, who angrily left the meeting room after our heated exchange. Preda attempted to rationalize the wrongs done to political prisoners by President Aliyev's intricate handling of the country's complex international affairs. That was plain outrageous. As an example, I brought in my conversation of 2002 or 2003 with Guillermo Martínez-Casañ, another PACE rapporteur on Azerbaijan. Whereas it was clear that the Aliyevs had been establishing a dynastic succession fortified by harsh repressions and no reform, Martínez-Casañ had frowned at me when I referred to one of the public speeches of Aliyev Junior: 'Mr Mammadov, you should pay attention to what he is doing, not what he is saying!'

It was my well-deserved turn to blow-off some steam at a PACE rapporteur telling me the same silly stuff ten years later when I was in prison in violation of the fundamental convention of the Council of Europe.

Schennach refrained from involving himself in our fight out of politeness. He always tried to be helpful as practically as he could, that is not only by formally reporting the political prisoner problem to the generally inert PACE, but also by doing something extra. Thanks to his efforts, the administration finally fixed my bed to alleviate my persistent back pain. On another day he came to the prison chief and said that if I was not given a chair with a backrest, he personally would buy one, bring it to the prison gates, sit on it until it was given to me, and invite all the journalists to report the action. I had had no access to a chair with a backrest for years, and this had increased my back pain. Schennach's attention made a real difference – not immediately, but gradually the administration started making such chairs more available for the inmates.

Stefan was also very kind to my wife Vafa during her trip to Strasbourg. A homemaker, never a public figure, in May 2017 she was invited to speak at a side event at another Council of Europe gathering. Her speech, in which she called on the Council of Europe to stop procrastinating, was perfect, and does not need my commentary.

An amusing story associated to that speech in her very good, but imperfect Russian sprang from a cultural incident in the introductory part. Vafa had consulted me beforehand on how to greet the audience. I advised her to start with 'dear friends' and then add 'respected' with reference to whoever she would see present in the meeting hall. She wrote in her notes 'Дорогие друзья, уважаемые…' (Dear Friends, Respected …), but in the end, due to the stress of public speaking, she accidentally forgot to replace the dots with a concrete reference. So without one, the introduction fully matched her key message, because in Russian, when you want to call on someone to be responsible in performing their duties you just call them 'уважаемые' ('respected') with a pause to follow. And yes, in her speech, she called on the Council of Europe to stop procrastinating.

In Strasbourg Vafa was impressed by the moral support she received from another Council of Europe official – Human Rights Commissioner Nils Muižnieks. When she stepped into his office, she noticed my painted portrait prominently displayed on the wall. She took a photo of the wall, and brought it to me. That was a nice gesture from Nils, although my inner optimist and cheerful ego were not particularly fond of that too sombre and dramatic piece of Scandinavian artwork. Overall, I felt pity that those caring and desperate Council officials like Nils were forced to act as civil society leaders, and not representatives of a prominent international organization. In addition, this demonstration of solidarity highlighted the inefficiency of the protections the key bodies of the Council were responsible for.

When in April 2018 he was succeeded by Dunja Mijatović, remembering my encounter with her shortly before all this mess had begun, I thought with irony that perhaps the portrait had now been removed from the office. During her visit to Baku in 2019, her assistant called me trying to schedule a meeting for us. I invited her to our office, but Mijatović said she was too busy, and insisted that I should come to whatever office she had in Baku. The seemingly insurmountable distance between the locations was only two kilometres by car. I declined the invitation.

Numerous civil society organizations worldwide tirelessly made public calls aimed at the deaf ears of Azerbaijani authorities – both as organizations, which was their primary occupation, and, in some instances taking the issue personally, like Jack Hanning, head of the Council of Europe affiliate network of schools of political studies. Jack had gone above and beyond everything by regularly sending letters to his British MPs. He urged them to make active inquiries to the British government about my case. This is a very brief description of his countless efforts. However, what could those dedicated civil society and individual efforts do when the most plenipotentiary organization was ready to accept the Azerbaijani government's procrastination game?

BEYOND CORRUPTION IN STRASBOURG

The government's intention was clear: it needed the procrastination in order to maintain the waves of fear it was instilling in society. I stood as a glaring testament to why individuals should not place their trust in Azerbaijan's international commitments if they aspire to challenge the government's policies.

But what had incapacitated the Council of Europe? One of my Strasbourg interlocutors once noted that the Council could not be better than the sum of its members. In other words, even if you are right, you still need to form a majority among members for action to be taken. That majority is impossible without at least one powerful country caring about the integrity of the system.

Essentially, for many years there had been no such country. Not least because there has never been a consolidated West in relation to Azerbaijan in general, and to the human rights issue in particular. The government consistently played favourites, offering huge economic benefits to one European country over another. It perpetuated the famous 'divide and rule' principle. Whenever the French got preferential treatment, the state TV channels screamed about the decay of Germany. Conversely, when German businesses were favoured, France was portrayed as a country to be despised. The leading position of British Petroleum in the oil and gas industry was a separate table in the government's simultaneous chess display.

THE HIGH PROFILES

Two months after being granted conditional release, I obtained a copy of a letter of reply signed by the chief of staff of French President Emmanuel Macron. The letter informed international human rights activists, including Rasul Jafarov and others, that President Macron had discussed the implementation of the European Court's judgment on my case with President Aliyev. Remarkably, this conversation took place in July, shortly before I was set free.

It was such a long and arduous way before someone truly prominent internationally could raise the issue with President Aliyev. Having served 80 per cent of my sentence, I was about to destroy the myth of the reliability of ECHR protections. Macron felt nothing particular about me. My early release could at least have saved face for the institution that offered us European protections. Their value has shrunk anyway, but face-saving has always been the most common practice in international relations.

At the end of 2013, during another break in the court sitting, I was casually chatting with a British diplomat who had come to observe the trial. While I was confined within a cage, people were allowed to approach, and shake hands. I mentioned to him my personal acquaintance with then UK Foreign Secretary William Hague. He immediately suggested I write to him.

Mr Hague replied with a very warm letter, and during his visit to Baku raised my issue with our foreign minister only, not with the president. Indeed, at the time when the European Court's judgment had not yet been made, who could tell that I wasn't a criminal? This revealed the level of confidence the authorities enjoyed in handling situations like mine: any sovereign government was a priori more credible than any of its opponents. Even the 13 years of Azerbaijan's deceitful membership of the Council of Europe, and our appalling human rights record had zero effect on the fundamental perception that government people are too serious to inflict upon themselves the reputational cost of a blatant lie.

William Hague and I weren't friends. We had met regularly at International Democrat Union events around the globe when he was chairman of that organization of centre-right parties in the early 2000s. So, without the European Court's judgment and five and a half years in prison, my case stood no chance of gaining attention at the heavyweight, political celebrity level.

THE ARMENIA FACTOR

Some international advocates for my freedom were driven by motives unrelated to sustaining the viability of the Convention system. Their engine was fuelled by their pro-Armenian beliefs, often poorly informed or irrational, but in some instances guided by the famous Diaspora. They just needed another drop of evidence to validate the continued military occupation of our lands. Such imitations of human rights activism became too obvious during the 2020 and 2023 military operations that restored the territorial integrity of Azerbaijan.

Partially, they were deluded by our own government's domestic propaganda, which had claimed that I would be soft on the military occupation issue because I was too liberal. The government lied on purpose. In the past, I had heard from government people only positive feedback about my attendance at such high-level conferences in Yerevan as Wilton Park and Rose Roth. Indeed, I spoke in Yerevan about the ethnic cleansing in my father's and grandfathers' homeland, West Zangezur, and other parts of present-day Armenia. At the time, the government itself could not afford to continually articulate these facts. Moreover, in 2005, I had loudly resigned from my consultant job at the International Crisis Group precisely because I disagreed with the organization's pro-Armenian report.

It is interesting in retrospect that in the early period of my detention, the pro-government propagandists in Europe and the US, including civil society activists and journalists, stuck to the opposite thesis – that REAL was an 'illiberal opposition'. That narrative was useful in the beginning, to confuse everyone, but was replaced down the years.

WITHSTANDING THE MARIONETTES

Back in 2013 and 2014 the government had already warned me: 'Если же нам придётся отпустить Вас без прошения о помиловании, мы спустим на Вас всех наших собак во власти, и в оппозиции'. ('And if we are forced to release you without a plea for a pardon, we will set all our government and opposition dogs loose on you.')

I was not only happy about my release, but also very proud of it. The government started to attack that feeling from my first press conference. The conventional pseudo-radical opposition, as well as other government assets within civil society and the 'independent' media, became instrumental in this onslaught.

Their chorus started chanting that I was against street rallies. Allegedly, I had concluded a secret deal with the government in exchange for my release, and my task was to discredit what Bolsheviks used to call the 'revolutionary activism of the masses'. This narrative was a centrally operated government effort, starting with a distorted presentation of my call for election preparations. 'True' opposition, to contrast this, vowed to change the government through massive rallies, whereas less than two years were left to the next parliamentary elections, and it was more logical to integrate rallies into whatever election strategy we chose as opposition.

The campaign was not limited to social media. Countless gossip-like reports to international circles served the same purpose. The government's intention in this operation was to scare me into submission. They expected me to cower in fear at the prospect of losing domestic and international credibility, and to surrender if they threatened another arrest, or at least to give up any further struggle for the full execution of the judgment.

All this commotion began when I reiterated our call to concentrate on elections instead of diverting opposition manpower to organizing wasteful street protests not aligned with the electoral timeline. This had been an established strategy of our REAL movement. We contended that election boycotts did not work, while mass mobilization ahead of the elections created an opportunity for change – either by ordinary parliamentary transformation or by higher than usual attendance at peaceful street protests aimed at ensuring the recognition of voting results.

This first wave of attempted discreditation broke on 18 January 2019, when I called on people to join a mass rally at three o'clock the following day against the new round of politically motivated arrests. The staggering 250,000 social media views of this call within less than 24 hours left the authorities feeling uneasy.

The probation agency demanded that I immediately appear in its office three hours before the rally. At noon I was there. Its chief asked me to withdraw the call and not to attend the mass gathering personally. I refused. Then he asked his staffer if I had signed the registration form every ten days in the past five months since conditional release. Unnerved by a positive answer, he locked me in a small office room in the same building. I was told to stay there till five o'clock, and then my fate would be decided.

I spent two hours practically under arrest. Suddenly, they changed their mind, and took me back to the chief's office. He repeated his demand. I made it clear that unless he formally forbade me in writing to attend the rally, I would not comply. Anything else would be against the law, and I would not obey such illegal orders. In the end, he snapped that I was free to go wherever I pleased.

Released only one hour before the rally, I finally spoke at the event. Though it constituted the largest state-authorized demonstration in many years, it was attended by only 15,000 people – certainly not sufficient to change the government, as my critics aspired to do, outside of the election cycle. Moreover, the government banned any future rallies, and none of my 'radical' would-be instructors dared to challenge the ban by action.

Instead, they launched a new attack narrative against our movement in April 2019 by claiming that two of our key figures – Erkin Gadirli and Natig Jafarli – had been sent to Brussels by the government with the aim of creating a reformist image for the ruling family. This wave of propaganda also crashed against the firm rocks of truth when it turned out that Natig and Erkin had been invited by an international NGO which the government had black-listed. The whole point of this smear campaign by the 'radical opposition' in the interests of the government was to force us to disclose the sponsor of the visit. We finally did so, reluctantly, but having duly informed the NGO in advance. The government learned what it wanted.

This was neither the first, nor the last act of cooperation between the government and the 'radical opposition' against us moderates.

This particular round of coordinated attacks served one more practical purpose, associated with the Article 46 § 4 infringement procedure. I am sure the government was aware of the direction the deliberations in the Grand Chamber of the

European Court of Human Rights were taking. The final deliberation, out of the four in total, took place on 1 April. Knowing that it was failing to sell my conditional release, and the subsequent removal* of conditions as an execution of the judgment, it needed to cultivate more public distrust towards the REAL movement ahead of the impending bad news. That is why all its resources within the 'radical opposition', 'independent civil society' and 'non-profit media' were mobilized for this crusade against us.

      Note*: One week before Erkin and Natig's controversial visit, the local appellate court changed the previous year's conditional release decision, thus removing all direct restrictions on my freedom, such as the travel ban, but keeping in force the indirect ban on standing in elections.

SUPPRESSION OF THE GRAND CHAMBER NEWS

On 29 May 2019, the Grand Chamber of the European Court of Human Rights finally delivered its judgment. According to it, by not executing the Court's judgment on my case, Azerbaijan had failed to fulfil its membership obligation.

Only people whom we as the Republican Alternative could reach through our organizational networks and social media were correctly informed about this unprecedented win. That was a substantial number, but certainly not enough. The government totally suppressed the reach, with the media barely covering the story. Social media outlets did not pick up the story either. Comments from otherwise vocal civil society lawyers were disappointingly scarce, and the driest possible. Supposedly independent news agency Turan wrote a bizarre article misrepresenting the issue at stake, extensively articulating the government's position, and ignoring the crux of the matter. When I called them to ask what was happening, I heard that it was a holiday, there was no good translator around, and therefore the editor-in-chief had personally reported the news relying solely on his limited proficiency in English and understanding of the law.

AIRBORNE

After the lifting of the travel ban, I could finally go abroad, namely to Strasbourg. While we were changing planes at Istanbul airport during my first flight in over six years, a well-trained chorus of American students started singing this song right in the transfer bus:

> Some may boast of prowess bold
> Of the schools they think so grand
> But there's a spirit can ne'er be told.
> We've got to fight boys
> We've got to fight!

I was absolutely delighted at the symbolism. It was a heart-warming and uplifting spectacle. Yes, I was going to continue fighting. People often say you have to live the moment, not capture it on camera for your social media account. I agree, and abide by that principle now. However, I had been disconnected from the Internet for so long and was so thirsty for such motivational surprises that I recorded and posted their beautiful performance online immediately (https://www.instagram.com/p/BxdAkWPDi9t/).

Another aviation surprise was that in the plane to Strasbourg I found myself seated in the first row of economy class, just behind business class, which was full of members of the Azerbaijani parliamentary delegation to PACE. I posted a photo of the separating curtain with a sarcastic commentary, guessing the amount of caviar they might be carrying in their baggage. I was in a good mood though: it was better to fly to Strasbourg in the same plane as Samad Seyidov, even with the class difference, than to shout at him vainly in Sheki prison in the presence of the PACE president.

FINALLY IN STRASBOURG

My meetings in Strasbourg were partly ceremonial, but I did present key points to my interlocutors, including Secretary General Thorbjørn Jagland, prominent members Frank Schwabe, Tiny Kox, Sunna Ævarsdóttir who was the rapporteur on political prisoners in Azerbaijan, and others. Besides, I had one big closed meeting with the permanent representatives of two dozen states, which had been pushing for the Article 46 § 4 infringement procedure. By coincidence, I came across the former PACE president, Anne Brasseur.

I had summarized all my key messages in a video interview with Radio Free Europe/Radio Liberty right there in Strasbourg. I thanked all the Council people for their solidarity, which probably helped me survive the difficult years, but reminded them that the Council had been created not with this minimalist purpose of keeping innocent politicians alive in prison. Its original purpose was to prevent such imprisonments in principle. Secondly, I underlined that after three conclusive victories at the European Court I refused to hear advice on any additional legal action: it was the Council who should take action so that I could run in the forthcoming parliamentary elections in 2020. I made this clarification, because the government now wanted me to write a request for the removal of the criminal record only, and the Council people were asking me questions about the prospects for it. I insisted on full acquittal.

The government continued asserting that I was not a politician even after my release. Just like in many other instances, it was convenient to some of its counterparts to accept this view rather than continue friction with the government. During my time in Strasbourg, Daniel Holtgen, the director of communications at the Council of Europe, approached me to ask if it was okay to share on Twitter the information about my meeting with Secretary General Thorbjørn Jagland. It was very kind of him to be concerned about my safety. I agreed, and he did post a photo and a text. However, when I saw the tweet, it said I was a 'human rights defender', not a damn politician. That was inappropriate, and I called him straight away. As you know from the reflections mentioned earlier in this book, this description did not match the challenging nature of the fight I had willingly taken on, a fight that has caused me great pain. However, Mr Holtgen refused to amend the text, and resorted to telling me fairy tales about human rights defender being a more respected title than political opponent of the government. I understood his motive, and did not press too much, but only out of courtesy. In reality, I was very upset by the perpetual cowardice of the Council bodies not willing to mess with authoritarian leaders.

MOVING FROM RESISTANCE TO PERSISTENCE

I stuck to the same line of argument as in Strasbourg in an extensive conversation with PACE President Liliane Maury Pasquier in Baku in September. She kindly invited me to a separate meeting, and listened with utmost seriousness. I highly appreciated her intelligent comprehension, because I had grown weary of the emotional takes of weak people underutilizing the Council's capacity.

A week later, in one of his farewell speeches Secretary General Thorbjørn Jagland reiterated that my release was only possible because he had pushed for the application of Article 46 § 4. This was true:

> 'Ultimately, our organization took the measure required. This included my use of Article 52 of the Convention, and, at my request, the Committee of

Ministers first ever deployed Article 46 § 4. I have no doubt that this played the major role in the eventual decision to end Mr Mammadov's detention, and it sent a powerful signal to all member states.'

However, one can feel here a hint of exasperation at the assessment of the Council's efforts in my 29 May online speech. I had made it at a closed meeting arranged by the European Implementation Network (EIN), a civil society organization dealing with matters related to the European Court of Human Rights. Furthermore, I had formulated similar messages during meetings in Strasbourg in June, as well as in subsequent statements for the press.

Well, having served 80 per cent of the original sentence, I had every reason to wonder why it took so long for the Committee of Ministers to apply the fundamental principle.

On 29 May, the EIN organized an online event for me to address the Strasbourg representatives of about two dozen 'like-minded member states'. Subsequently, in June, and again in January 2020, I met with them in Strasbourg face-to-face, for continued in-depth conversation. These were mostly the countries that had been pushing for Article 46 § 4, although a few of them had doubts about it and were generally inclined to value their relations with the government of Azerbaijan higher than the Convention.

At those events, having expressed all my gratitude for their solidarity, I was outspoken and critical about the permanent procrastination by the Council. The government was fooling the organization, and the latter was accepting this game as if it could not decipher the intention.

I explained why the execution of the judgment ought to go beyond just setting me free and erasing my criminal record by providing full exoneration. Not everyone could know that the devil lay in the details of our Constitution.

The judgment of the European Court required what is called 'restitutio in integrum' in Latin – restoration of my pre-arrest situation to the best extent possible.

In some countries or in application to some people, 'restitutio in integrum' may be limited to release from detention and erasure of criminal record. Our government wanted to impose universal recognition of this limited interpretation on the Committee of Ministers, and it could potentially do it, given its strength at the Council.

I categorically objected. Prior to the arrest, I could run in both parliamentary and presidential elections. The elimination of my post-prison criminal record would restore my right to be a parliamentary candidate. However, the criminal record reservations for presidential candidates were written in the Constitution in a slightly different wording, leaving room for misinterpretations to disqualify anyone who has ever been convicted.

If I agreed to the closure of the case without acquittal, then one day, in the heat of a presidential race, the government could bluntly disqualify me under the Constitutional provision, without reasonable time to re-open the case at the Committee of Ministers, and achieve rectification.

My persistence created additional strain between the Council of Europe and the government. While the Council could not disagree with me, it also aimed to preserve its 'cooperation' with the authorities. I created a real headache, which the Council people did not expect. They had wanted some respite after my release, but they weren't getting it.

I was pressing on all fronts. In September, before Jagland's farewell speech, I met in Baku not only with the PACE president, as mentioned earlier, but also with Sunna Ævarsdóttir, rapporteur on Azerbaijani political prisoners. I repeated for her the constitutional dimension, and the main points of my most recent August appeal to the Committee of

Ministers (per our usual practice, I wrote it, and my lawyer formally sent it to the Committee):

> 'These findings perfectly correspond to the long years of warnings the applicant has made to the Committee of Ministers that the authorities of Azerbaijan will do everything possible to procrastinate the process to the point of full public discreditation of the Convention protections, and effective ban on the applicant's participation in the presidential or parliamentary elections as a candidate.'

In January 2020, in the middle of the campaign for snap parliamentary elections, I flew to Strasbourg again, where I had two decisive conversations.

One was with Christos Giakoumopoulos, the Council of Europe's director general of human rights and rule of law. That exchange was extraordinarily easy. We spoke absolutely the same legal language, although he mostly listened. He agreed with virtually every single argument I presented.

Reflecting on the meeting, I was sarcastic about myself, 'Where could I be so wrong that I was so right in the conversation?' I joked with friends who were also at the meeting that you hear so much affirmation of your views when you are totally dumb. The future developments demonstrated that it was not me that was dumb, but the system that had caused so much suffering to people.

The other key meeting was with Sunna Ævarsdóttir again. The draft PACE resolution based on her report called for the restoration of my right to be a parliamentary candidate in elections. Though it was not her intention, the call conflicted with what I was arguing for – full exoneration so that I could be a presidential candidate as well. To solve the matter, I asked her to remove the word 'parliamentary' from the draft. We agreed that two members of the Assembly would make the proposal, and she, as a rapporteur, would support the proposal during the plenary session. Let us see how the debate at the plenary session unfolded on 29 January:

> Mr Andreas Nick, President of the Assembly: We come to amendment number 3 and I call Mr Stefan Schennach to support amendment number 3.
>
> Mr Stefan Schennach: We want, with this amendment, to delete the words 'the forthcoming parliamentary'. These three words. Because we made a statement that it is not acceptable that Mr Ilgar Mammadov cannot run and others also not. The Azeris has to fulfil the Human Rights Court's decision and it's not only for the forthcoming parliamentarian election. It has to do in principle.
>
> Mr Andreas Nick, President of the Assembly: Does anyone speak against?
>
> Mr Samad Seyidov: This is actually a very strange amendment, and I think that the forthcoming elections are really very important and this is another attempt to some kind of influence to this election. And that's why I'm not in favour to keep this kind of amendment. And that's why I'm completely against. Because we are on the eve of the forthcoming parliamentary elections.
>
> Mr Andreas Nick, President of the Assembly: What is the opinion of the Committee?
>
> Mr Boriss Cilevičs: The Committee was in favour.
>
> Mr Andreas Nick, President of the Assembly: I should now put the amendment to the vote. The vote is open... The vote is closed... The amendment is adopted.

A week later, on 5 February, speaking to Turkish Foreign Minister Mevlüt Çavuşoğlu, who had actually been PACE president for two years up until January 2012, I learnt that President Aliyev had harshly criticized the PACE resolution: 'For us it has no more value than a piece of paper. We do not accept any of the far-fetched accusations contained in it and will not fulfil any of their "requirements".'

President Aliyev kept his word. I could not participate in the parliamentary elections conducted a few days after his exchange with the Turkish minister. Moreover, in violation of the Constitution, he decided not to hold elections for ten out of a total of 125 parliamentary seats, which for various reasons remained vacant between 2020 and 2024. This denied political representation to hundreds of thousands of citizens, but the goal of not fulfilling the resolution was achieved: how could I run in the absence of elections?

Well, I skipped the snap presidential elections in 2024 because President Aliyev's rearrangement of the sequence of the polls to bask once more in the glory of the 2020 war victory rendered any opposition challenge futile. Our support for him during the war had showcased national unity. The subsequent parliamentary and municipal elections were meant to reveal his plans for the country post-victory: if nothing improved fundamentally, then I would energetically challenge his vision in the contest for the presidency. However, by conducting snap presidential polls first, he transformed the race into a conversation about the past, about his outstanding role in the recent military victory, and not about the future.

Let's go back to 2020 for now. One week after the parliamentary elections I called all the people onto the streets in protest at the falsification of the results. Hundreds were forcibly put on buses and driven far away from the capital city of Baku. I myself was abducted by people in plain clothes, and put in a car with police number plates.

This happened in broad daylight on a central street. Luckily my supporters were broadcasting the attack live on social media. That saved me from being beaten up again. I was unaware of that broadcast while on the road, driven 200 kilometres away from Baku. That was scary, because I could not know what orders these guys had been given. Hours later, they freed me on a highway 30 kilometres from Baku.

Today, more than four years since the incident, my application about it, sent by lawyer Javad Javadov, is still pending in the European Court. Communication between the Court and the government has not even started yet. I can easily imagine the mood, 'Abduction by our member government? Oh, no, save us from another headache.'

DIALOGUE

Shortly after the failed kidnapping operation, the government invited me to what it called 'political dialogue'.

Actually, the kidnapping was the last drop of absurdity in the government's distrust towards us as a political player: at the elections, we had nominated 29 candidates, and won several seats, two of them confidently, but the government allowed REAL to occupy only one seat, thinking that we would reject the seats if recognized. This nonsense was taking place against the backdrop of my numerous calls for dialogue, which had fallen on deaf ears in past years.

When the government finally noticed our steadfast enthusiasm for engaging in meaningful political conversation, combined with our consistent refusal to succumb to intimidation, it finally responded with the cautious and limited initiative for political dialogue.

In spring and summer, I met several times with the newly appointed department chief of the Presidential Administration who was in charge of liaising with the Parliament and political parties.

Beyond a broad exchange of views on the potential for political relaxation in the country, we also delved into various practical matters concerning that agenda. Among them was the Article 18 group of cases under the review of the Committee of Ministers of the Council of Europe. At the time, it concerned 12 individuals, of whom four, including myself, were members of the Republican Alternative.

My insistence that all 12 judgments should be executed first if we wanted to be confident about our intentions was not received too well initially, but while we continued talking, the government gradually showed more readiness to proceed with the execution – of seven judgments as a first step, and then of the rest.

When it came to practicalities, the administration always sought a formal excuse in the independence of the Supreme Court as a branch of power. To this I responded tactfully that by hiding behind the non-existing separation of powers they would keep us suspicious about their plans forever. Yet, their tactics did not prevent them from requesting and readily receiving updates about my formal moves at the Supreme Court.

At one point they were surprised at how small a sum I requested in compensation for moral damage – only 127,000 euros. This number was my subjective extrapolation of the amount awarded by the ECHR for the first 9 months of detention to the rest 57 months. I explained that there were many cases in the Article 18 group, and if I set a precedent with a particularly high level of damages, that would disrupt the fragile tendency within their government towards resolving the outstanding cases. My primary goal was to set a precedent for Europe by getting full acquittal as a result of the Article 46 § 4 infringement procedure. Money was a secondary issue.

Speaking of money, lawyer Fuad Aghayev refused to request compensation for me directly from the Supreme

Court. He argued that the established practice was to achieve an acquittal at the Supreme Court, and then, on that basis, request compensation at the lower court. Again, I had to study the subject myself, and write a detailed legal description explaining that nothing prevented the Supreme Court from assigning moral compensation directly. I was not sure about compensation for material damage though. In the end, the Supreme Court agreed with my view. Thus, I pioneered another legal practice, which many people benefitted from after my case. The Supreme Court awarded the moral compensation directly, but the issue of material damage was passed to a lower court, where it got buried after several trials: both the district court, and the Appellate Court rejected my claim for compensation for material damage. Tired of the endless and distracting legal process, I did not climb further up the judicial pyramid, and decided just to move on.

In 2020 the task of not harming what could potentially become the nascent opening within the government was extremely difficult for a particular reason: the officials who had been instructed to orchestrate all the repressions against us, and bore responsibility for the complete failure of associated judicial proceedings remained extremely powerful, cunning and vengeful. Not that they were inherently worse than the other elements of the system, they just had a personal motive to disrupt the potentially emerging process. If a sudden surge in acquittals were to occur, it would not only expose their incompetence, but also mark them within the system as out of favour with the president.

Partially they succeeded. While we expected resolution of all seven cases at the Supreme Court as a package, on 23 April, as a first step, we achieved only two acquittals and one termination of criminal prosecution. All three cases were about the REAL leadership – Rasul Jafarov, Natig Jafarli and me.

That was a triumph by any account. However, the country was under a strict pseudo-medical lockdown. People were allowed to leave their homes only if they received permission electronically and only for two hours a day. Therefore, we could find no space to celebrate the victory on the scale its grandeur deserved.

ICARUS

During my time at school, around the age of 13 or 14, I had a nickname I hated: Icarus. My best friend Albert Pinkhasov coined this moniker because it sounded like my name, but was easier for him to pronounce. Several times I told him to stop teasing me, because to other people Icarus was familiar not as a character in ancient Greek mythology, but as the Hungarian-made urban buses that traversed the streets of Baku. We even had a fight, but he continued needling me all the time. Then I stopped paying attention to his antics, and the nickname gradually disappeared by the end of high school.

People have a lot of time to ponder in prison. When I recalled the Icarus story of my teenage years, I chuckled at the irony of unsuspecting Albert being so prophetic about the future I was going to face. In this tale, picture Daedalus, symbolizing the Council of Europe, who crafted a magnificent pair of wings. These wings, in the form of Convention protections, were meant to be my salvation from years in the labyrinth of prisons. However, instead of handing them over to me, Daedalus found himself endlessly flirting with the Minotaur, the government.

Both before and after my release, I constantly reminded myself that unlike the mythical Icarus, I had to follow the flight instructions and avoid flying directly towards the Sun. That was the only path to a complete judicial victory, and now I am proud of having achieved it.

The prison time experience of interactions with European officials had only convinced me that many of them would feel happily relieved of moral duty, if after my conditional release I were to engage in a reckless strategy of street rallies against the government, and end up behind bars again. I had been convicted for organizing an insurrection, literally, and therefore, if I were to give any chance to the government to argue that my intention to overthrow the regime by force was real, a number of influential Council of Europe people would simply wash their hands of the matter, saying, 'Well, we did what we could, but it is your own fault this time, you should have behaved after your release.'

Such people would not outnumber, but would definitely outperform the people of principle. Same applies to the member governments. This is the clearest impression I have of the totality of my interactions and conversations with Council of Europe representatives over the years 2013-2020.

www.ingramcontent.com/pod-product-compliance
Lightning Source LLC
Chambersburg PA
CBHW031925240526
45464CB00022B/947